The Jacobite Invasion of 1745 in the North West

JONATHAN D. OATES

Centre for North-West Regional Studies
Lancaster University
2006
Series Editor: Jean Turnbull

The Jacobite Invasion of 1745 in the North West

This volume is the 53rd in a series of Occasional Papers published by the
Centre for North-West Regional Studies at the University of Lancaster

Text Copyright © Jonathan D. Oates 2006

Designed, typeset, printed and bound by
4word Ltd, Bristol

British Library Cataloguing in-Publication Data

A CIP catalogue entry for this book is available from the British Library

ISBN 1-86220-179-X

Contents

Acknowledgements

Christopher Duffy in *The '45* is right to observe that 'Every passably serious historical study is inevitably a joint enterprise'.

First of I must thank Her Majesty the Queen for permission to quote from the Royal Archives. I must also extend my thanks to those archivists who have assisted in my quest for significant amounts of archival material; in particular those at Carlisle, Kendal, Chester and Preston, but also those at the British Library and the National Archives.

This work would not be in print were it not for the editor of the series, Dr Jean Turnbull who read through the drafts, made corrections, supplied most of the pictures and much more besides. I also thank the librarians, museum curators, archivists and latter day Jacobites who helped identify and supply most of these images

Dr Stephen Taylor read through part of an early draft and Eveline Cruickshanks also read through a draft without noting anything too erroneous, as well as supplying me with a number of relevant *Royal Stuart Society Papers*.

My father, David Oates, took the three pictures of Clifton which feature here.

Peter Lole, Richard Sharp and Geoff Wilson were also kind enough to supply and allow the use of relevant photographs, and the Thoresby Society likewise to allow the use of one of their pictures.

I would like to thank my wife, Caroline, for her help and encouragement in the researching and writing of this book.

Any mistakes made herein are, of course, mine alone.

The book is dedicated to my brother, Matthew, Shirley and Freya, who live in Scotland.

Illustrations

Maps

Introduction

If eighteenth century British history, sandwiched between the Civil War and the Napoleonic War, has been generally neglected, there is one episode which is evergreen. Indeed, since 1746 histories have always been in print and this trend does not seem likely to abate. Novelists, film makers, television and the tourist industry have also taken notice of this topic, which is, of course, the attempt by the Jacobites to seize the throne in 1745. 'Bonnie Prince Charlie', the Duke of Cumberland and Culloden are all as evocative as ever.

This has often been viewed, and to an extent still is, as an episode of Scottish history. This book does not aim to be yet just another account of that campaign. It is not concerned with Charles Edward Stuart (1720–1788), or the marches and battles of the campaign, except as a background. Rather, it sets out to focus on the activity of the men and women of north-west England, the counties through which his forces marched in November and December 1745. The definition of the north west to be used hereafter is that of the four pre-1974 counties of Cumberland, Westmorland, Lancashire and Cheshire.

A note about the terms used. Although the terms 'rebellion' and 'rising' are often employed when describing this event on the national level, it would seem that from the point of view of the north west of England, that the term 'invasion' is better, as the Jacobite army marched into the region in November 1745, rather than there being any spontaneous uprising, and sympathisers joined or welcomed them from within. Instead of being referred to as Prince or Pretender, Charles Edward Stuart is termed Charles throughout. Apart from direct quotations, his followers are called Jacobites, rather than rebels. The armies of George II are referred to as regular troops, not Hanoverian, English or British. This is to try and avoid the use of loaded terms which contain bias, intentional or otherwise.

This introduction's purposes are six-fold. Firstly it briefly explains the background to the Forty Five. The second, and by far the largest section, concerns the political, economic, social and religious significance of the north west. Thirdly the historiography of the campaign of 1745, with special regard to the north west, is surveyed. By seeing what has been written hitherto, the reader is alerted to the current state of historical knowledge and debate. Fourthly, the sources for this new study are examined. Fifthly, an outline of the contents is laid down. Finally the issues which are raised throughout the work are discussed.

The national background to the events of 1745

In order to understand Charles Stuart's attempt to take the throne of George II (1683–1760) and to replace him with his father, the exiled James Francis Stuart (1688–1766), we need to recall the events of the previous half century. In 1688, James Francis' father, the Catholic James II (1633–1701), had been expelled from Britain by the forces of the Dutch, but Protestant, William of Orange (1650–1702). William and his wife, James II's eldest daughter, Mary (1662–1694), were declared joint monarchs (as William III and Mary II) by Parliament in the following year. Because they were childless, the Crown passed to James II's other legitimate daughter, Anne (1665–1714), after William's death. Anne reigned from 1702–1714 and was to be the last of the Stuart monarchs.

[Figure 1] 'Prince Charles Edward Stuart', engraving by Robert Strange, published c.1745. Richard Sharp's collection.

The last of Anne's children died in 1700. The Act of Settlement, passed in 1701, declared that after Anne's death, a granddaughter of James I, Sophia (1630–1714), dowager electress of the small German duchy of Hanover and her successors, would inherit the Crown of Great Britain. Sophia predeceased Anne by a few weeks and so when Anne died on 1 August 1714, Sophia's son, George Lewis, Elector of Hanover (1660–1727), was pronounced King George.

This succession, as outlined above, did not go smoothly. James II and later, his son, were determined to reclaim the throne which they were certain was theirs by right of hereditary succession. A significant minority – at the least – of their former subjects throughout Britain agreed with them. They were known as Jacobites, from Jacobus, the Latin for James. From 1689 until the later eighteenth century, there were a number of plots,

[Figure 2]
George II. Reproduced by permission of The Thoresby Society
(The Leeds Historical Society),

invasion attempts and internal efforts made to restore them. Britain's enemies, notably France and Spain, often aided the Jacobite cause when it was in their interest to do so.

During William III's reign there were short wars in Ireland and Scotland to restore James II. There were even invasion plans and assassination plots against William in England. All these were eventually defeated. When James II died in 1701, James Francis had been recognised by both France and the Jacobites as the titular James III. Anne's reign was generally less troubled by the Jacobites, but there was an abortive invasion attempt in 1708. During George I's reign, serious insurrections broke out in both England and Scotland in 1715, but these were badly managed and were once again crushed. Another attempt in 1719 also failed. Plots later in the reign were centred around the Swedish Ambassador, Count Gyllenborg in 1717 and Francis Atterbury, bishop of Rochester in 1722, but were also unsuccessful. In 1727, George I died and was peacefully succeeded by his son, George II. Domestic support for the exiled Stuarts seemed largely dormant.

QUÆRIT PATRIA CÆSAREM.

[Figure 3]
'King James III', an anonymous etching after Francesco Ponzone, published 1747. Richard Sharp's Collection.

However, this was misleading. For the Stuarts, there was a new hope. In 1719 James Francis had married Princess Clemetina Sobieska and the union produced two sons; Charles Edward (known to history as either 'Bonnie Prince Charlie' or the Young Pretender) and Henry (1722–1807). With age, James showed less interest in actively pursuing the throne, but Charles was of another mind. In 1744, following an invitation by a number of southern English Jacobites, he had been ready to sail with a French invasion force. Bad weather foiled the bid, but he was not daunted and was to make another, more well known attempt, in the following year.

The north west of England

It is important to understand a little about the geographical, social, economic, religious, political and military background to the region of England whose inhabitants are under discussion. The four north-western counties of England formed a geographical entity, making up as they did a bloc north from the border of Scotland as far south as the north-easterly borders of Wales and the Midlands. On the west they were bordered by the Irish Sea and on the east with the Pennines. This was a relatively thin strip of land compared to the broader north-east region of Yorkshire, Northumberland and Durham. Cumberland, Westmorland and northern Lancashire were hilly and mountainous, before the lower lying land in the south and west of Lancashire and Cheshire was reached. The easiest route through the hilly regions was along the road from Carlisle to Lancaster, via Penrith and Kendal, or vice versa, not from west to east.

The two northerly counties were thinly populated, whereas Lancashire was the most populous. In 1700, Cumberland had between 60 and 65,000 residents; Westmorland a mere 27 to 30,000.[1] At the other end was Lancashire with approximately 160 to 180,000 inhabitants. Cheshire's population was between that of Cumberland and Lancashire.[2] Liverpool was the largest town in the region, with 22,000 inhabitants in 1750 followed by Manchester with over 10,000. Other large towns included Chester, with a population which was slightly less than that of Manchester; Whitehaven with perhaps about 7,000 and Carlisle with only 4,000.[3] However, most of the inhabitants of these counties lived in small towns and even smaller villages and hamlets which were not even mentioned by contemporary travel writers.

Some of the towns in the north west were major national centres of commerce. Liverpool was the most important. Being coastal, it benefited from trade with Ireland, the American colonies and Africa. In 1687, more ships had entered Bristol than Liverpool, but by 1764, Liverpool's incoming traffic had doubled that of its southern rival. As regards outgoing tonnage,

[Figure 4]
South prospect of Preston. Reproduced courtesy of Lancashire Library and Information Service.

THE SOUTH PROSPECT OF PRESTON, IN THE COUNTY PALATINE OF LANCASTER.

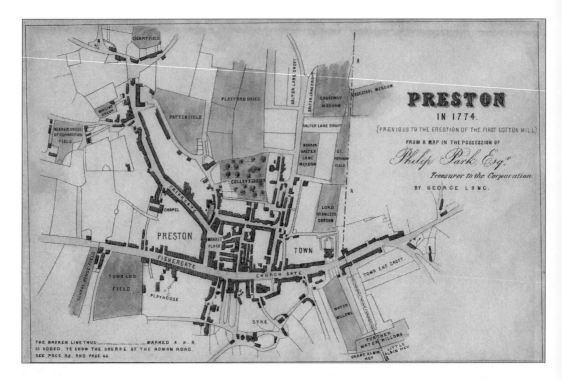

in 1750 Liverpool was fourth in the country with 42,662 tons.[4] Liverpool was described as 'one of the wonders of Britain…The town has now an opulent, flourishing and increasing trade…increasing every way in wealth and shipping'.[5] Another major commercial town was Manchester, a rising centre of the textile industry in the county. Smaller towns in Lancashire, such as Wigan, Bolton and Bury also manufactured cotton.[6]

Less commercially successful were Preston and Lancaster. The former was a major social centre 'full of attorneys, proctors and notaries…Here is a great deal of good company'.[7] Although Daniel Defoe, in his famous *Tour* published in 1724–1726 thought Lancaster was in a state of decay, the Rev. Robert Patten wrote that it was 'a Town of very good Trade, very pleasantly seated' and boasting of a sea port.[8]

The most northern counties were least conducive to human inhabitation. Defoe wrote that Westmorland was 'a country eminent only for being the wildest, most barren and frightful of any that I have passed over in England, or even in Wales'. Though Kirkby Lonsdale and Kendal produced textiles, Appleby's position was less happy. According to Defoe, it was 'once a flourishing city, now a decayed and half demolished town'.[9]

Cumberland, though, was a different story. It produced more coal than any single county, except the far larger Yorkshire, with 350,000 tons being extracted in 1750.[10] The conduit for this coal was Whitehaven. Its outgoing tonnage was, in 1750; second only to London with 100,778.[11] Penrith was an important market town in the county, Carlisle being less so.[12]

[Figure 5]
Plan of Preston, 1774. Reproduced courtesy of Lancashire Library and Information Service.

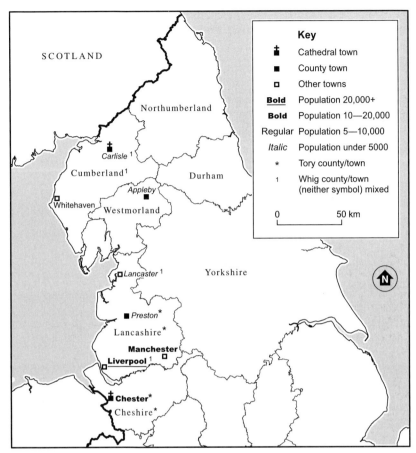

Key

✚	Cathedral town
■	County town
◻	Other towns
Bold	Population 20,000+
Bold	Population 10—20,000
Regular	Population 5—10,000
Italic	Population under 5000
*	Tory county/town
1	Whig county/town (neither symbol) mixed

0   50 km

[Map 1]
Map of the North West of England showing Parliamentary loyalties, 1741–1747. Map drawn by Simon Chew.

Cheshire was not known for its industries as the other counties were, but rather for its agricultural produce, as befitted a flat county. Defoe estimated that about 22,000 tons of cheese went from here to London and other English counties, as well as quantities to Scotland and Ireland. He went on to remark:

> this cheese manufacture…increases every day, and greatly enriches all the county; raises the value of the lands, and encourages the farmers to the keeping vast stocks of cows.[13]

Administratively, there were a number of jurisdictions in the north west. Each of the four counties, as other counties throughout England, had its court of Quarter Sessions, made up of country gentlemen who were the Justices of the Peace (JPs). They met four times a year to deal with a variety of offences. More weighty matters, such as treason and murder, were dealt with by the Northern Assize circuits, which were held twice annually, and also covered Yorkshire and Northumberland. However, to complicate matters, both Lancashire and Cheshire were palatine jurisdictions, which meant that they possessed their own courts and tried serious offences outside the Assize circuits.

The titular secular head of each county was the Lord Lieutenant, the King's representative in the shires, a territorial magnate who was also politically important in his own right. In times of emergency, he and his deputies dealt with matters relating to the militia. But instead of the north western counties possessing one Lieutenant each, Cumberland and Westmorland were under the remit of a single Lieutenant; Cheshire and Lancashire, more conventionally possessed one apiece. They were assisted in their work by deputy lieutenants, taken from the ranks of fellow noblemen and gentry.

Politically, the north west, as with any part of England, was divided. Parliament was split between Tories and Whigs, neither of whom were anything resembling a united political entity. The Tories had not, in general, enjoyed royal favour and political power since the accession of the Hanoverian dynasty in 1714. Some had inclined themselves towards Jacobitism, but by no means all. As for the ruling oligarchy of Whigs, they were far from being a united 'party' either, and many of the party conflicts in this period were

[Figure 6]
Todd's Map of Kendal, 1787. Reproduced by permission of Cumbria Archive Service.

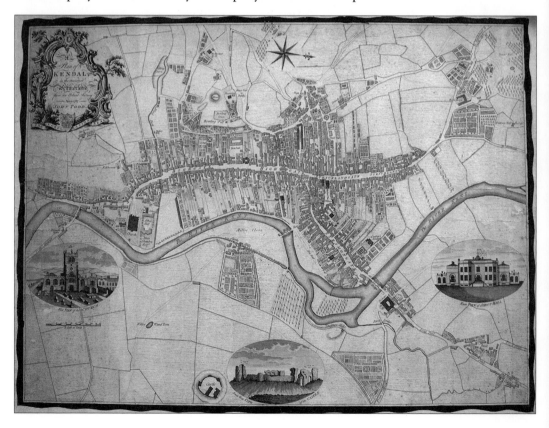

between different factions of Whigs. Generally speaking, the Whigs were in favour of the Hanoverian Succession, to varying degrees whereas Tory allegiances were less clear. Each county and each ancient corporation returned two MPs to Parliament, regardless of population or wealth.

Those MPs who represented Cumberland, Carlisle and Cockermouth in 1745 were all Whigs. Sir James Lowther (c.1676–1755) an MP for Cumberland, was one of the wealthiest men in the north west, indeed, the country, with a fortune made in the coal trade. In Westmorland, both the county and the corporation of Appleby were split, each having one Tory and one Whig member. Lancashire and Cheshire were more inclined towards the Tory interest; all Cheshire MPs being so, and 10 out of 14 Lancashire MPs were Tory. The four Whig MPs in the county represented Lancaster and Liverpool, which were strongholds of the Dissenting and commercial interests.[14]

Some of these constituencies were uncontested, especially where men of the same party orientation were concerned. Where men could not agree, there would have to be an election. The most recent contest had been in 1741. These had been held in Carlisle, Westmorland and Preston. Such elections, when they did occur, involved many men; all these constituencies had over 500 voters, so political interest, controversy and division were not restricted to a few noble and gentry families.[15]

Most Englishmen were members of the Church of England, as established in the sixteenth century. The north west was divided between two bishoprics. That of Carlisle was made up of all the parishes in Cumberland and some of those in Westmorland. That of Chester included Lancashire, Cheshire and part of Westmorland. Pastoral care in the larger parishes was often thought to be weak, especially where populations grew and clerical strength was limited. Bishops were men of political significance and, at parish level, the clergyman was a man of some importance. Generally, the Church of England supported the status quo in Church and state, as it guaranteed their authority. A Catholic Stuart monarch would, it was feared, put that power in jeopardy. Protestant England often saw itself as in peril from the larger Catholic powers. There were also a minority of Anglicans who were known as non jurors, men and women who did not acknowledge any de facto monarch since 1689 as head of the Church of England, recognising the descendants of James II instead. A strong community existed in Manchester and so were a potential support to any Jacobite invasion.[16]

In religion there was a great deal of diversity between the different counties in the north west. There were a few gentry families who were of the Catholic persuasion in Cheshire, Cumberland and Westmorland, but the situation was far different in Lancashire. This county had the largest Catholic population in England outside London; perhaps a tenth of the population were Catholic. Some of these were Irish immigrants, but many were old and established Catholic families. There were rather more

Dissenters; perhaps five per cent in Cumberland and Westmorland were Presbyterians and three to four per cent were Quakers; there were also Dissenting strongholds in Liverpool and Lancaster.[17] Members of these religious groups were denied the full fruits of civil society. Dissenters could legally worship, but Catholics could not, though in practice it is probable that de facto toleration often occurred. None could hold civil or military office. Yet Dissenters, eager to cling to their limited rights, were mostly pro-Hanoverian, whereas Catholics had more to gain from Jacobitism, who advocated wholesale religious toleration.

The north west of England, and Lancashire in particular, had played an important part in previous attempts to restore the Stuarts. In part this was because of the strength of Catholicism in Lancashire. Under the Catholic James II, the county nobility and gentry had prospered, being given what had been denied to them since the Reformation – positions of trust under the Crown in the locality. Catholic gentlemen became Justices of the Peace and deputy lieutenants. In 1687–1688 the Lord Lieutenant was Catholic – a great honour. The penal laws had also been relaxed. However, after the Revolution of 1688 all this changed. The Catholics lost their positions of authority and the penal laws were reinstated. This led to plotting in the county to reinstate James II, and in 1694 a Jacobite plot was discovered. Yet, though the conspirators were acquitted, the plot had been genuine enough.[18]

Catholic Lancashire had supplied a relatively large number of recruits to the Jacobite cause in 1715 when Thomas Forster led a Jacobite army south from Cumberland. At both Lancaster and Preston, Catholics joined in numbers. An eye witness observed that at the latter 'Here they were also joined by a great many Gentlemen, with their Tenants, Servants and Attendants, and some of very good Figure in the Country; but still all Papists'.[19] Catholics, then, were feared as potential supporters of any attempt to restore the Stuarts. This was more so in 1745 because Britain was at war with the two principal Catholic powers of Europe, France and Spain, who, it was feared, would support any Jacobite attempt.

Support from other parts of the north west was limited – from Cumberland 22 joined; five came from Westmorland and three from Cheshire. However Lancashire supplied 396 men and possibly many more. These figures merely number those taken in captivity, for probably many more joined but escaped before the final surrender.[20] The potential for Jacobitism in Cheshire was indicated by the county's Jacobite Club, based at Ashby Hall, which voted by the narrowest of margins – one vote – against action at this time, though the club was far from defunct in the 1740s and was known as the Cheshire Cycle Club. There was, reputedly, another Jacobite club based at The Plume of the Feathers at Chester in 1723. There were also Jacobite drinking clubs in Lancashire, too: one at Rochdale and another at Walton le Dale. In all, it has been estimated that there were eight such clubs in Lancashire and three in Cheshire in 1745; though none in

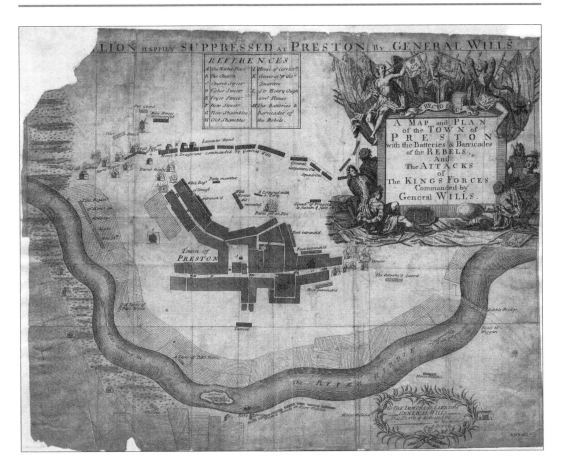

REFERENCES

A	The Market Place	I	House of Correct
B	The Church	K	General Wills'
C	Church Street		Quarters
D	Fisher Street	L	Sir Henry Ough-
E	Fryer Street		ton' House
F	New Street	M	The Batteries &
G	New Shambles		Barricades of
H	Old Shambles		the Rebels.

A MAP and PLAN
of the TOWN of
PRESTON
with the Batteries & Barricades
of the REBELS,
And
The ATTACKS
of
The KINGS FORCES
Commanded by
General WILLS.

[Figure 7]
Plan of the Battle
of Preston.
Reproduced
courtesy of
Lancashire Library
and Information
Service.

Cumberland and Westmorland. How far these were dens of active conspiracy is questionable. The evidence is naturally limited and in any case, conviviality was a prime concern of these clubs.[21] The Jacobite attempt in 1715 was crushed at the Battle of Preston, and some later paid with their lives – would this result in a desire for caution or for revenge should another opportunity present itself to Jacobites of the next generation?

But there were also those in the north west in 1715 who opposed the Jacobites, though not always effectually. The sheriff of Cumberland gathered the county posse near Penrith to block their march and the bishop of Carlisle joined them. However, on the news of the Jacobite arrival, they fled.[22] Some tax collectors ran away rather than give up their funds to the Jacobites; clergy refused to pray for James Francis.[23] At Liverpool, companies of volunteers were formed and defences erected. Sir Henry Hoghton (1679–1755) raised the county militia of Lancashire and two Dissenting ministers raised their flocks against the Jacobites.[24]

Others in the north west took a more neutral approach to the invading army. Tax collectors gave up the money in their hands to the Jacobites. At Lancaster, the townsmen were reluctant to destroy the bridge which might have hindered the Jacobites' march. The Vicar there hedged his bets; according to Patten 'he wanted to see how the Scales would turn, before he could think of venturing so far'.[25]

Militarily, the region was exposed. In previous centuries the towns closest to Scotland had been attacked, but border warfare had disappeared since the union of Crowns in 1603. True, armies had marched through in the district in the latter stages of the Civil Wars, in 1648 and 1651, and there had been the invasion in 1715, with two battles at Preston in 1648 and 1715. On the whole, though, this was as peaceful a part of England as any. The only longstanding military presence were the garrisons in the castles of Chester and Carlisle, but these were weak, and in Carlisle's case, the governor and his deputy were absentee. In Chester, the matter was helped by the Lord Lieutenant, George Cholmondeley, the third Earl of Cholmondeley (1703–1770), who was also the castle's governor. Although the civilians who made up the county militia were meant to be exercised every year, and their arms kept in order, they seem to have been neglected here as elsewhere in the kingdom. It should be recalled that eighteenth century England was a society in which military knowledge and use of arms was limited, and hence was particularly vulnerable to invasion if robbed of its professional army, as it was in war time; in 1745 Britain was at war with France. This should be borne in mind when determining how effectively civilians could take part in any combat scenario.

Thus, administratively, politically and religiously, the people of the north west were divided. There was little homogeneity or common foci for loyalty – certainly the King, who was a remote figure in London (or in his native Hanover), was not an obvious one. How they would react to an intruder was difficult to discern. With such a history of divided responses towards the Jacobites in 1715, it was a wise man who could successfully predict the behaviour of those in the north west in 1745.

The north west was important at this time because it was the region of England which the Jacobite army marched through in 1745 in both directions. If it were to receive the support they envisaged it would have to be from these counties, for it would have been relatively easy for men to either enlist or to show their enthusiasm for a second Stuart restoration in less militant fashions. On the other hand, if there was to be any civilian resistance, it would have to manifest itself within this region if it were to be effective. Activity in these four counties also reveal a cross-section of how the civil administration, social and religious groups reacted to a military invasion within their very midst.

Historiography

There are two types of history of the Forty Five which concern us here; those dealing with the national issues, either the campaign of the Forty Five or with Jacobitism on a national level, and secondly, those dealing specifically with the north west and the Forty Five. Until relatively recently, although the north west has featured in every history of the Forty Five, the role of its people has been relatively neglected in favour of the military forces marching through the region. Thus we read of the town and castle of Carlisle falling without much struggle to the Jacobites on 15 November 1745. Then, with the Jacobite march southward, inhabitants appear as mere spectators, neither resisting nor joining the Jacobites. At Manchester, however, Jacobite fortunes change as about 200 men joined their cause. After the retreat from Derby, responses became more hostile as the country people attacked retreating Jacobite stragglers. Then the Manchester recruits formed part of the garrison at Carlisle and are forced to surrender to their pursuers on 30 December. Such an account, seen as it is from the view of the Jacobite invaders, is grossly unfair and simplistic, but it was the rule, at least as recently as the mid-twentieth century, as recounted by a noted Jacobite scholar, Sir Charles Petrie.[26] Those periods of time before the armies marched through the north west and after they had traversed these counties have traditionally been ignored by those looking at the matter from a purely military view. To do so, however, ignores much evidence as to the political and religious sympathies of those concerned.

Books about 'Bonnie Prince Charlie' and the campaign itself have never been in short supply. However, general histories of Jacobitism and the Forty Five became more prolific from the 1970s. Professional historians began to view the subject more carefully and produced a number of major studies. The best accounts of the military campaign of the Forty Five are Speck's *The Butcher* and Reid's *1745*, which give pro-government views of the crisis, whereas Black and McLynn give pro-Jacobite perspectives. These were superseded, perhaps, by the best single account to date, which also has the advantage of impartiality. This is Duffy's *The '45*. This is a detailed account of the campaign which gives fresh insights to an oft told tale. It can be highly recommended to anyone wanting to read a good history of the struggle.[27]

Other historians have examined Jacobitism in England. Eveline Cruickshanks was the first to do so, and described Tory involvement in Jacobite conspiracies in the events leading up to 1745. Another important book is Paul Monod's *Jacobitism and the English people, 1689–1788*, first published in 1989. He surveyed the phenomenon of the English Jacobites in its social, cultural, religious and political milieu. English Jacobites, including those of the north west, from 1689–1788, were discussed in order to illustrate the multi-facetted nature of English Jacobitism. More disappointing was Evelyn Lord's *The Stuarts' Secret Army*, which also concerned English Jacobites, but had little new to say.[28]

Another important work about England was by Frank McLynn, who wrote the only book solely to study the campaign of the Forty Five in England, focussing, day by day, on the months of November and

December. His prime concern, of course, is of the commanders and their armies on both sides, but there is some consideration given to the quasi-military activity of volunteer and militia bodies within the north west. On the whole, though, this work does not show that they were particularly effective.[29]

The examination of the English dimension of the Forty Five in the north west has largely been the work of Rupert Jarvis. Jarvis was primarily an economic and social historian, but wrote a number of excellent articles about the impact of the Forty Five on the organs of 'local government' in the north west of England. These were published in academic journals from the 1940s to the 1960s, but, fortunately from the viewpoint of the modern historian, over a score of them were republished in two volumes under the title, *Collected Papers on the Jacobite Risings*.[30]

Jarvis was the first to examine the archives held by Cumberland Record Office (as it then was), and to a lesser extent, the archives of Lancashire and Cheshire, as well as those of the Public Record Office (as it then was), the British Library, the contemporary press and contemporary narratives. No historian has done so much work in this field. Jarvis concentrated on some topics which were obviously specific to the north west, such as the Manchester constables and the impact of the invasion as regards Liverpool. He also explored more general topics, such as the questions concerning the militia and the recusancy laws, using examples taken from the north west to illustrate his argument.[31]

Apart from these articles, Jarvis also put together a volume of extracts from the Cumberland Lieutenancy and Quarter Sessions archives concerning the Jacobite Rebellions of 1715 and 1745. Both these, and the lengthy introductory guide, are invaluable to the scholar.[32] Yet, and this is not to detract from Jarvis' labours, he was not all-inclusive. He wrote virtually nothing about the Anglican Church, for instance. Nor did he do much to examine the north-west Jacobites themselves.

Purely local studies are variable. One of the best known is Mounsey's book on Carlisle which has been heavily relied upon by successive writers, though it as much a collection of material for a history rather than a history in its own right. [33] In the early twentieth century there were two books about the Forty Five in Cumberland and Carlisle, which support the behaviour of the defenders of Carlisle in face of both the Jacobites and an unsympathetic government in London. Both rely heavily on previously published sources. [34] The popular Dalesman series produced a *Jacobites in Lancashire* in 1971. Although not without interest, this slim booklet covers both the Fifteen and the Forty Five, and is of limited value. [35] Far better is Don Higham's *Liverpool and the Forty Five*. As the work of an amateur historian, it is of immense use, drawing as it does on a variety of sources and supplanting Jarvis' article on the city. [36] Roger Turner's booklet about Manchester in 1745 discusses the Jacobites in that town, though not their opponents. [37] Chester and Cheshire's story in this period seems to have been largely neglected except for Smith's booklet, which studies the campaign of the Forty Five and its impact on the north west and references in the *Victoria County History* series.[38]

Articles about the Forty Five have been printed in county history journals since the late nineteenth century, chiefly in the *Transactions* of the Cumberland and Westmorland Antiquarian and Archaeological Society, far less so in those journals devoted to Cheshire. Again, these have been variable in nature. Some of the better ones examine the chief incidents of military history. The Chancellor of Carlisle wrote an even-handed account in 1889 of the skirmish at Clifton Moor and more recently there have been articles about the transporting of siege artillery towards Carlisle in December 1745 and another about the siege of that place in the last ten days of the same year.[39]

Despite all these works, one thing is clear. There is no one general account of the responses of the people of the north west towards the Jacobite invasion of 1745. Most have concentrated either on one facet of it, or have presented the individuals therein as part of a larger canvas. The aim of this book is to tackle this oversight.

Sources

In order to investigate how the people of the north west reacted in this time of crisis, we now turn to the sources for the study of the impact of the Jacobite invasion in England.[40] Here we specifically examine those sources concerned with the north west. As with any history, the sources are both numerous and widely dispersed. No historian attempting to uncover the history of any region, can realistically hope to find all the information in one place. There are three main classes of primary sources (as opposed to the secondary sources – books and articles written by historians after the time of the events they are studying): archives of central government; archives created and collected by local government and published primary sources. These were all written down at the time of the events they describe, or shortly afterwards.

The most single important institution for archives concerning British history is The National Archives at Kew (formerly the Public Record Office). This houses the archives of central government, and within these archives is much material of interest to those concerned with local history. As regards the Forty Five the State Papers Domestic, series 36, covering the reign of George II, are of paramount value. These include letters written to and from the principal Secretary of State for the years 1745–1746. This was Thomas Holles-Pelham, Duke of Newcastle (1693–1768). His correspondents include magistrates, clergymen, merchants and soldiers, and some of these were based in the north west. They sent invaluable reports about the state of the defences in their counties and the loyalty or otherwise of the populace. Newcastle, in turn, gave the government's response concerning that assistance which could be given to them, instructions, and his advice as to what to do. Other important sources at the National Archives are judicial papers; those of King's Bench, Assize records, Palatine archives and the papers of the Treasury Solicitors, all of which provide details of men accused of Jacobite activity.

Other London-based sources are the Newcastle and Hardwicke Papers at the British Library and the Cumberland Papers housed at Windsor Castle, but available for reference elsewhere on microfilm. The forementioned Newcastle and Philip Yorke (1690–1764), Earl of Hardwicke and Lord Chancellor, wrote voluminously in this period and there is much in their correspondence about the progress of the invasion and the activity of those in the counties in opposition to it. George II's younger son was William Augustus, Duke of Cumberland (1721–1766) and as Captain General, he was given the responsibility, in November 1745, of leading the regular forces in the suppression of the Jacobites. He received correspondence concerning the military details of the campaign and this, and his replies, are copious.

Then there are the archives housed in the north west. Most of these are in the possession of county and municipal record offices. These are composed of the archives of the predecessor authorities of the county councils; chiefly the county Quarter Sessions, and a miscellany of both parish archives and those of individuals associated with these counties. The Quarter Sessions archives tell what the official response of the counties were, and they include the steps taken against local Catholics and Jacobites, more general security measures and efforts to assist the regular troops. Corporation minute and account books tell a similar story for their jurisdictions. Parish archives, chiefly churchwardens' and less commonly, constables' accounts, indicate what was done at parish level, such as loyalist bell ringing and providing men and arms to the county militia. Other archives to be found here are the correspondence of prominent gentry and noblemen, especially of those such as Henry Lowther, third Viscount Lonsdale (1694–1751) and Edward Stanley, the eleventh Earl of Derby (1689–1776), the Lords Lieutenant, respectively, of Cumberland and Westmorland and of Lancashire. These tell of fears and measures taken against the Jacobites.

Finally there are the published sources. These can be subdivided into two categories. The first are those which were written and published at the time. These include the few sermons of the Anglican clergy which were preached and later published – chiefly as loyalist propaganda both during and after the Forty Five. Then there are the newspapers, both national and local. The only surviving copies of any regional newspaper are those of *The Manchester Magazine*. Other contemporary prints are those of the last speeches of north-western Jacobite officers taken and hanged in 1746. Finally there are the contemporary or near contemporary histories of the rebellion, all of which include, to varying degrees, sections concerning activity in the north west – albeit often taken from the press, and all written in favour of the government.

The other key sources are the memoirs and diaries of contemporaries which were published from the nineteenth century onwards. Some are those of observers in the north west. The most famous and well used is the diary of Elizabeth Byrom, daughter of a Manchester Jacobite, John Byrom. Less well known accounts are by one of the Manchester constables, by Dr Richard Kay of Bury and the Rev. George Williamson of Arthuret in Cumberland. These give accounts of both the diarist's own actions and thoughts and his or her perceptions of others' behaviour. A number of Jacobite officers wrote memoirs of all or part of the campaign of the Forty Five. These have been well used by historians of the Forty Five, but as all discuss the march south and/or the retreat after Derby and comment on the reactions in the north west, they cannot be ignored by the regional historian. Although all were on the same side, they all interpret events differently and so provide conflicting evidence.

None of these sources in themselves can tell the whole story. Each tells part of the story and then only from one particular angle. Biased, inaccurate, exaggerated or plain wrong as many of these are, taken together, they can be examined and interpreted in order to give a coherent and balanced account of what happened in the north west as far as it is possible, at this distance of time, to do so.

Structure

This book seeks to show a new light on the Jacobite invasion of England of 1745. It does not seek merely discuss behaviour in the north west during the Jacobite army's march through England from 9 November – 21 December, but follows through responses from the first reported news of Charles' arrival in 1745 to after his final defeat in the following year. There was a medley of responses from all sections of state, Church and society. None of these groupings are hard and fast. After all, the nobility, clergy and gentry made up the ranks of the Lieutenancy and the JPs, the middling people were members of the corporations, and Catholics could come from any social grouping.

Therefore the decision has been taken to present the story in a chronological fashion, divided into four main chapters. The first considers the responses in the north west in the months leading up to the Jacobite invasion. It concentrates on the activity of those loyal to George II; chiefly the Lords Lieutenant and their agents, the corporations of Carlisle and Liverpool and the Anglican Church, as well as the views and actions of the people of these counties. This is because almost all the surviving evidence concerns them; little space is devoted to the Jacobites of the north west because there is so little known of their hopes and activities at this time.

Chapter Two is an account of reactions to the actual invasion in November; divided between those in Cumberland and Westmorland, those in Lancashire and lastly, those in Cheshire. This reflects the fact that the Jacobite army marched through these counties in that order. Here there is much space dedicated to the Jacobites of these counties because there is more evidence for their behaviour, as they now had the chance to show their devotion, in a number of fashions, to the cause. Loyalist responses, based on what already had happened and the immediate Jacobite military challenge, are not neglected either.

The third chapter considers local activity in the following month, when the Jacobite army was in retreat, pursued by the regular forces. This is divided as in the previous chapter, but in reverse. The last chapter discusses both the immediate aftermath of the invasion in 1746 and the longer term impact of Jacobitism and its opponents in the north west during the reigns of George II and III. Responses to local events, such as the fall of Carlisle, the arrest of local officials and the trials of prisoners, and to more distant events, such as Culloden, are also explored. The longer term survival and decline of Jacobitism, in its different manifestations, is also outlined.

These chapters also sketch the decisions and movement of the armies as the background to the activity in the north west in order that local reactions can be properly understood.

Issues

Finally, we need to touch upon the issues which this book examines. These are points which have been raised, though not always answered, by historians in previous works. The prime question is to tackle the issue to which most historians of the Forty Five either explicitly or implicitly refer: that is to say, the state of England. How did Englishmen respond to the Jacobite invasion? Most historians conclude that, given that few Englishmen joined the Jacobites, they were not supportive of Jacobitism. But they also state that since little effectual resistance was made to the Jacobite army as it marched southwards, that they were not particularly enamoured of the Hanoverian status quo either. As Jeremy Black, perhaps the most prolific author on eighteenth century British history, has noted 'The Jacobites who claimed that Britain was ready to rise in revolution were to be proved wrong in 1745, but equally the Hanoverian regime was revealed as having a very narrow base'.[41]

Some attention has been paid towards attitudes in the north west, but only in a sketchy fashion. Some historians have poured scorn on those who were, apparently, supportive of George II. McLynn, for instance, wrote:

Naturally, great stress is laid by pro-Hanoverian historians on the copious professions of loyalty before the invasion of England. But there is not much evidence of this crucial loyalty in the crucial month 8 November – 5 December 1745. What is certain is that all 'loyal' forces set up to oppose the clansmen melted away with amazing rapidity once the prospect of a real fight loomed.[42]

Black agrees, writing:

it was their passive position on the march south that was crucial. Neither side appeared to have enjoyed the enthusiastic support of the bulk of the population, certainly to the extent of armed action.[43]

A discordant note is struck by William Speck:

Yet this in itself is no measure of his [Charles'] acceptability to people in England…It is not altogether surprising that the amateur garrison at Carlisle, hastily scratched together from the local militias, capitulated when they learnt that they could not expect any help from Wade's army, and were threatened with fire and sword if they refused.[44]

Similarly, Colley notes:

hardly any civilians who were not Roman Catholic joined it [the Jacobite army]. True, very few civilians acting on their own initiative attempted to physically stop it either. But those historians who put this inaction down to indifference need to think again. English civilians at this time had no adequate militia training and only limited and usually obsolete firearms, Unless they were very brave or very stupid, therefore, they were hardly likely to take pot shots at an army of Highlanders and risk reprisals.[45]

As to the Jacobites themselves, although few actually enlisted, pro-Jacobite historians do not see this as evidence of a lack of Jacobite sympathies. Monod writes, 'If a willingness to die for a cause were the only true indication of resolve, then very few Englishmen or women in the modern age have been seriously committed to anything'.[46] Likewise, Pittock writes 'Within groups who held such [Jacobite] beliefs, rioting and enlistment in Jacobite armies, was, as is surely always the case in politics, the role of a minority of activists amid a mass of sympathisers: the tip of an iceberg'.[47] These historians stress that those who were sympathetic towards Jacobitism showed their faith in other ways; culturally, religiously and socially and argue that those Jacobites who did not take up arms should not be dismissed as mere sentimentalists. A more cynical view is expressed by Szechi:

The Tories were basically faint hearts whenever serious action was in prospect, but there was always the chance that a foreign power impressed by their transient zeal might invade, and even draw large numbers of Tories into turning out to fight – if it looked like winning.[48]

It is interesting to note that those sympathetic to Jacobitism are sympathetic to those 'Jacobites' who did not turn out to fight, but scorn their opponents who acted in an equally cautious manner. The same can be said of the pro-Hanoverian historians; ridiculing the cautious Jacobites, whilst excusing the behaviour of their opponents who often did not fight either. It also has to be said that none of the historians above have examined the north west in detail and thus have been prone to make generalisations about the state of activity there based on a relatively cursory survey of the evidence (they, after all, were concentrating on a larger canvas, namely the whole campaign or Jacobitism from 1689–1788). We shall return to this debate later.

Since the success of the invasion depended to a large degree on support in England, this was a crucial question for all concerned with it. This book examines the people in that part of England who had plenty of chances to show their feeling towards both sides, demonstrating which of these opposing viewpoints has the greater veracity.

But there are other issues. The effectiveness, or otherwise, of that part of the British state in the north west is examined. There is little doubt that the eighteenth century state was powerful and successful in exerting its influence overseas, given the number of wars won and colonies gained. At home, however, it has been argued that it was a different story, with the central government exerting a very limited degree of control over various levels of provincial administration. Could a state operate effectively with such a degree of regional autonomy? The Forty Five was an example of seeing to what extent this loose 'system' would work in reality.

Toleration of religious minorities is another issue brought up at this time of national crisis. As mentioned above, the different denominations enjoyed, or endured, differing states of protection and discrimination. Since James Francis Stuart was Catholic, religion played an important part, though his supporters tried to downplay this and its opponents encouraged anti-Catholicism. How much discrimination was practised and how much individuals suffered for their faith in this period is another question to be explored.

Most important of all, though, are the people of the north west, men and women: rich and poor; Protestant and Catholic, Whig, Tory and Jacobite. Without them there would be no history to relate. How they thought, felt, spoke and acted is at the heart of this book. The marching of warlike armies was a novel experience for many of them (though some would have witnessed the march of armies, though on a far smaller scale, in 1715) and, at the least, an unsettling one. Faced with a situation which many of them did not relish, they had a variety of choices before them. These choices would depend on where they lived and who they were. For Jacobites this was, perhaps, an opportunity to aid the Jacobite army, though not necessarily so. For their opponents, this was a chance of showing their loyalty to George II and resisting the Jacobites. For others, the options were to lie low, to flee or to take other action.

It is their story which is told in the following pages. It is worth noting that, before any judgement is passed on contemporaries' behaviour, we must not judge them with hindsight. No one knew what the outcome of Charles Stuart's bid for the throne would be. If men were cautious, then perhaps those with no firm convictions, but personal and political security, were right to be so. Moreover, those who did speak or act on behalf of Hanover or Stuart, did so, not knowing which side would win, but despite personal risk, sure in their convictions.

CHAPTER ONE

Prelude to Invasion:
September – October 1745

Charles Edward Stuart arrived in Scotland in July 1745 and raised a small army of Highlanders. They took Edinburgh, defeated an equally miniscule regular army under Sir John Cope at Prestonpans on 21 September, and, it was feared, would march southwards into England. This did not occur at once; as men and money had to be raised, giving time for those in the north western counties (as elsewhere) to formulate their responses. The government was in the process of withdrawing its regular troops from the Continent in these months. The first substantial force was mustered at Newcastle upon Tyne under Field Marshal Wade (1673–1748) in October. The second was to be led by Sir John Ligonier (1680–1770) and was destined to march towards Staffordshire. Thus, the north west of England was to be bereft of a field army, at least at first, and therefore was left, to an extent, to its own devices.

Unsurprisingly, there was a great deal of concern about the possible Jacobite incursion. Lowther wrote to the Duke of Newcastle on 24 September, just after the news of Cope's defeat was known, 'The county [Cumberland] being next to North Britain was exceedingly alarmed when the Highlanders marcht from Perth…There not being one troop or company of His Majesty's Forces in this county except two companies of Invalids at Carlisle'.[1] Likewise, Thomas Pattinson, deputy mayor of Carlisle, wrote, only two days later, with the same sentiments, 'This extream nakedness makes me greatly fear the bad consequences'.[2] Yet there was no military assistance which could be sent, as Newcastle informed Pattinson on 3 October, 'in the present circumstances, you must be sensible that cannot be done'. Nor, except in the case of Liverpool, could any half-pay officers be sent to help train the militia.[3]

Activity within the north west in opposition to the Jacobites was very much in evidence in these months, especially in October. This was partly stimulated by central government, who issued forth directives about security measures to be taken and empowered the raising of forces. However, it was uncoordinated; those in the counties corresponded with the government, but not, as far as is known, with one another. The county authorities, principally the Lords Lieutenant and the magistrates, were certainly busy in the forming of militia and volunteer units, and in raising men and gathering arms for such. Suspects were monitored and moves taken to tabulate Catholics. Elsewhere, the agents of the Church were inculcating loyalty into their parishioners. Others looked on the scene with alarm, mortification or indifference.

Jacobitism and Indifference?

Before turning to the official and personal responses in the counties, it is worth examining the level of Jacobitism evident in the north west in these months. After all, the Jacobites expected assistance from their friends in northern England. A survey of noblemen and gentry with Jacobite sympathies in these four counties in 1743 listed 17, mostly Tories or dissident Whigs of Lancashire and Cheshire, though by 1745, three had died. [4]

The most prominent of these was James Barry, the fourth Earl of Barrymore (1667–1747), a leading Tory peer, who had a seat in southern Cheshire. In 1743, a Jacobite agent, John Murray, had written, that although some of the Tories:

> were very timorous, others such as Lord Bar[rymo]re very ready to join in any thing that could conduce to forward the Restoration, and that he frankly offered, when they proposed a sum of Money to be ready to the Value of £12,000 which was scrupled at by some, to provide it himself.[5]

Barrymore and others did send a sum of money to the Jacobites on the Continent in 1744.[6] However, Murray later claimed that Barrymore, along with the other leading Jacobites 'would not do anything unless a sufficient Body of Troops were landed from France'. We should note that Barrymore was 78 in 1745 and that in the previous year had stated that he would not risk his estates on any pretext.[7] Such caution was understandable – a foreign army had been needed to overthrow James II in 1688, but the purely domestic revolt in 1715 had failed, ending in the execution of some of its protagonists. We shall hear more of Barrymore in the next chapter.

Yet this did not mean that there was no Jacobite activity in these counties prior to November 1745. It was, however, very minimal. The Cumberland JPs examined at least two suspects who were deemed to have been potential Jacobites. News that a potentially seditious letter had been intercepted led to warrants for the arrest of two men being issued. On 26 September, the two, David Campbell and Richard Jackson, were questioned about a letter that the former had sent to the latter, as it contained phrases which seemed to suggest that the two were Jacobites. Both denied the charges, and were bailed for attendance at the next meeting of the Sessions Court; £500 for Campbell and £1,000 for Jackson.[8] At the beginning of November, five

Cumberland JPs questioned a Scot, John Henderson, who was thought to have been a spy, and committed him to Carlisle gaol.[9]

Indeed, in Cumberland, Lonsdale was confident that few would join the Jacobites, writing on 9 September, 'In such parts of the country as I have seen, there does not appear any Disposition of the people to favour the Rebellion'.[10] He later noted 'In general that there appeared a zeal and Readiness in contributing to the support of His Majesty's Government that exceeded the most sanguine expectations'.[11]

There was only minimal evidence for Jacobitism in Lancashire prior to November 1745. Although there were rumours that Manchester Jacobites had celebrated Cope's defeat, that a Jacobite paper had been seen and that there were seditious cries at night, yet another report claimed these were 'entirely groundless' and that Manchester was 'peaceable and well affected'.[12] However, another report, from an anonymous writer in Manchester to Sir Rowland Winn of Yorkshire on 14 September, put matters in a stronger light:

> It is with no small concern that I am obliged to inform you that the Disaffection of some in this part of the Country is but too notorious & should the Rebels march this way (which I hope will be prevented) I fear they will meet with too many friends...The passing of the Highlanders over the Forth...fills us with some apprehensions... Some marks of Joy & Hope very evidently shew themselves, & the topics of absolute monarchy & hereditary Right (which was also grateful) are now more resumed than before among us. These you will think shew the Inclinations of people, and perhaps their intentions, if Opportunity furrows.[13]

Suspicion that Jacobite sympathies were widespread persisted. Derby told Newcastle, on 22 September 'We have many papists in these parts...they are perfectly quiet, but how far things may alter...your Grace will best judge'. He added that, apart from the Catholics, 'there was never less appearance of an intention or a desire to disturb the government'.[14]

There were certainly a great many fears expressed about possible Catholic support for the rebellion among the defenders of the status quo. In early September, Dr. John Waugh (1703–1765), Chancellor of Carlisle, feared 'a few poor papists' might join Charles.[15] Sir Henry Hoghton believed the balance of force in Lancashire was pro-Jacobite 'We have some friends but few in comparison to those against us...I have not one gentleman I can discourse freely with on the subject but it would soon be as common as a newspaper'. He added 'As to our own County, our enemys are as strong as then [1715]' and that should the Jacobites arrive in Lancashire, there would be a rising on their behalf.[16] Lieutenant Robinson told Colonel Yorke that it was thought the Jacobites would march to Lancashire 'where we have too much reason to think they will find a good Catholic county, ready to join them'.[17]

There was also a report of Jacobite meetings among the Cheshire gentry in the summer months. One Mrs. Hatrell told Lord Baron Parker that meetings were held in country houses and at taverns in Chester where 'it is publickly reported by the servants &c. that the Pretender's health was constantly drunk &c.' Among those present was Barrymore. A gathering lasting five days was held at Thomas Longville's house, when all the women were sent away. There were also regular meetings at Hawarden. Whether this was evidence of conspiracy or not, it did look suspicious.[18] Cholmondeley feared that if the Jacobite army reached Cheshire 'I but too much apprehend their being joined by great Numbers' and made reference to the 'disaffected in the country'.[19]

Yet, despite these fears, little occurred to justify them in this period. This should not be surprising: with the Whigs in the ascendancy and no friends in sight, it would be a very daring Jacobite who would reveal his creed in public as this was an offence in the eyes of the law, punishable by gaol, a fine or a whipping. Yet the contrast between the very public outbreaks of Jacobite rioting in Lancashire in 1715 with the more cautious behaviour in 1745 was very marked.

Although Jacobitism was muted, loyalism towards George II was limited until, paradoxically, after the King's forces had been routed at Prestonpans and the rebellion's potential was made clear. There were few reactions of any kind to the outbreak of the rebellion in Scotland until late September. This was probably because it simply did not occur to many that it might impinge upon their lives – after all, the Fifteen was 30 years ago and a distant memory at best. Yet some did take notice. In August, Waugh discussed the sharing of intelligence with Lowland Scots magistrates in August, should it be necessary to do so.[20] An early warning which was sent to the government came from Owen Pritchard, mayor of Liverpool, to Newcastle on 16 August, alerting him to the arrival of the Charles Stuart.[21] Hoghton also wrote letters concerning the rebellion in Scotland from at least 1 September.[22] The anonymous writer of Manchester noted as early as 14 September that Derby 'though not so well with the Ministry as might be wished, yet Loyal to the Government, & ready to exert himself....Sir H. Houghton at Preston, Mr Horton of Chadderton near Manchester with many others, are very zealous & active in His Majesty's Interest'.[23]

Similarly, Richard Kay, a Dissenting Lancashire doctor, made the first reference in his diary to the rebellion on 24 September, only after hearing the news of Prestonpans, though he noted 'About 6 weeks or 2 months past we have been often hearing of a Rebellion in Scotland'. He implored God's help 'notwithstanding the Sins that are committed amongst us' and that they would be preserved from 'Popish slavery and vain Idolatory'.[24]

The only newspaper being printed (for which copies survive) in the region was the Whiggish *The Manchester Magazine*. It had a few references to the rebellion in August and September. It printed the proclamation for Charles Stuart's arrest, followed by notices of troop movements in Scotland.[25]

The Lieutenancy and Civil Defence

The initiative and the authority for most of the local action, however, came from the centre. On 5 September, the Privy Council sent decrees to all the Lords Lieutenant in the north of England. These acquainted them with the fact that Charles had arrived in Scotland, gathered followers in armed rebellion and had proceeded to attack a detachment of the regulars. The Lieutenants were ordered to confiscate the arms of all Catholics, non jurors or other suspected persons. Furthermore, the Catholics were to be summoned and then take oaths swearing their loyalty to the King and the Church of England, and of their abhorrence towards Charles. Any who refused could be confined to their homes and have their horses taken from them.[26] As well as the implementation of the recusancy laws, the lieutenancy were instructed to 'cause the whole Militia of the said County to be put in a readiness fit for immediate Service'.[27]

The Lords Lieutenants' prime duty at this time was civil defence. The counties had two traditional methods to raise forces. Firstly, there was the county militia, in which the Lord Lieutenant led local levies which were raised and officered by county landowners and equipped by the parishes. Derby did not have a high opinion of them 'I am not ignorant of the difficulty of raising the militia of the county, nor have I any great opinion of their usefulness in their present undisciplined state'. [28] Then there was the posse comitatus, a force of the county's able bodied men, led by the county sheriff. Yet the county shrievalty seem to have been largely inactive in 1745, so this second method was clearly a non-starter.

So much for theory and orders from London. Yet the raising of the militia was fraught with problems. Such were the forces of political inertia that civil defence had been neglected for many years and so the militia could not be legally embodied. This was because the Militia Act had expired in 1735. This had made it possible to raise men and to arm them without the necessity of the government reimbursing landowners the sums of money they had advanced towards maintaining them. Without a new Act of Parliament, therefore, civil defence in the counties was all but impotent. Most of the Lords Lieutenant were not prepared to break the law.[29]

The lack of weaponry was a difficulty which was also commonly acknowledged. Lonsdale wrote on 9 September 'Their Arms are extreamly bad and it is impossible to gain new ones in so short a time as they shall probably had'.[30] Of the 282 men who are definitely known to have made up the regiment of Foot Militia of Cumberland and Westmorland, 57 lacked a sword, seven were without a musket, 14 lacked a bayonet and nine lacked arms of any kind. Even of those who had weapons, almost half of those with muskets had faulty guns and 72 of the swords carried were also in poor condition.[31] The same was evident in Lancashire, with Derby claiming that there were but 20 muskets in the county.[32]

Derby thought that the militia would not be suitable as they were untrained, inexperienced and without suitable officers.[33] Few men had wanted to accept commissions. This was in part because there were few Protestant gentlemen as many of the county's gentry were Catholic. Indeed, Derby only knew one Whig gentleman who might make a good officer.[34] Cholmondeley did not expect to raise many men because of the stories spread by the 'disaffected' to deter volunteers.[35]

Another difficulty was the calibre of the Lieutenants themselves. Some, along with their deputies, were physically fragile. Newcastle wrote thus to Derby 'I am sorry to hear that your lordship's state of health is not so good.'[36] Derby later reported that he had 'a body jaded almost to death and an aching heart'.[37] Lowther wrote that he was similarly afflicted 'being of a great age and much disabl'd in my limbs with the gout'.[38] Lonsdale was absentee throughout the crisis and Hoghton was elderly. None had any military experience.

Many of the Lieutenants were, then, understandably gloomy about the prospects which lay before them. Lonsdale wrote as early as 9 September that 'very little service can reasonably be expected from the militia…I am afraid your Grace will find the militia in the other northern counties much in the same way'.[39] Similarly, Hoghton noted as early as 11 September 'if the Rebellion comes nearer us tis possible the disaffected amongst ourselves may rise, and we are defenceless if either that should happen'.[40] Derby thought that if the regulars arrived before the Jacobites, the militia would be superfluous to requirements; if vice versa, the militia would be unable to deal with them. In either case, their being raised was pointless.[41]

However, despite misgivings, the Lieutenancy did their best to act. In Cumberland and Westmorland the law was flouted and the Militia was summoned into being. Lonsdale, whatever his failings, certainly tried to comply with the instructions he had been given. It was, however, a rather lengthier process than it need have been, for his correspondence from London had to be sent to him at his Yorkshire seat at Byram, where he remained during the crisis, and then be sent by him to the requisite officials in Cumberland and Westmorland. Even so, on 9 September, he sent the Privy Council's order to Thomas Simpson of Penrith and Richard Wordsworth of Appleby, Clerks of the Peace, respectively, to Cumberland and Westmorland. They were to be the liaison agents between Lonsdale and the deputy lieutenants of each county and would be Muster Masters to the militia forces raised there. They were also given blank commissions for the men who would become militia officers. They were to attend meetings of the deputy lieutenants and report back to Lonsdale.[42]

When he wrote to the deputy lieutenants on 9 September about the raising of the militia, Lonsdale was frank as to the difficulties involved. Although he expected them to raise the Horse and Foot Militia of the two counties, he was aware of the problem of arming them. 'I am afraid [they] will prove defective and in bad Order, but you will require them to procure as good as can be had upon such an Emergency'. He wanted to see an account of the arms that had been found and also that there was sufficient ammunition for such arms that could be located.[43]

In Cumberland and Westmorland, the legal difficulty outlined above seems to have been overlooked. Newcastle, on 21 September, gave Lonsdale permission to form men into troops of militia in order to evade the Militia Act.[44] Lonsdale went along with this and reported to Newcastle on 24 September that his deputies 'have proceeded in this service with great chearfulness'.[45] Yet, after the first month of the militia's service was up, Lonsdale realised that they could not legally be kept together, and reminded Newcastle that 'I could advise them to nothing which was contrary to law'. Although he had already broken the law, he felt that some propriety should be observed.[46] He was not alone in this. The deputy lieutenants were concerned that the month's pay given to the men would expire in seven days time and so they would have to disband the militia. They told Lonsdale that this 'may be of ill consequence, and therefore we beg your Lordship's advice'. Lonsdale, in his turn, told Newcastle he was uncertain what to suggest and wanted Newcastle's help.[47] Newcastle told Lonsdale that 'I am persuaded your lordship will do everything in your power to prevent' this but did not tell him how it should be done. However, the militia was maintained until the capitulation at Carlisle, Lonsdale remarking 'They have been kept up much longer, than they would have been kept up in the regular way'. Apparently the militia officers ordered the clerk of the peace to raise the necessary money.[48]

The officers of the Cumberland and Westmorland Militia were men of local standing but not necessarily of any military background. Their colonel was Sir John Pennington, baronet and deputy lieutenant. The junior officers were gentlemen and esquires.[49]

Apart from the possibility of raising the militia, there was, in 1745, another way of forming men into units to defend the state, and to avoid the legal difficulties associated with the militia; that of associations, where the King granted commissions through the lieutenancy and corporations. In this instance volunteers were raised and financed by loyal subscriptions, though officered as with the militia. On 20 September, Newcastle alerted Derby to the danger posed by the rebellion and suggested raising forces to oppose it. He acknowledged that the militia might be a dead letter due to legal difficulties and that to raise forces by association might be most

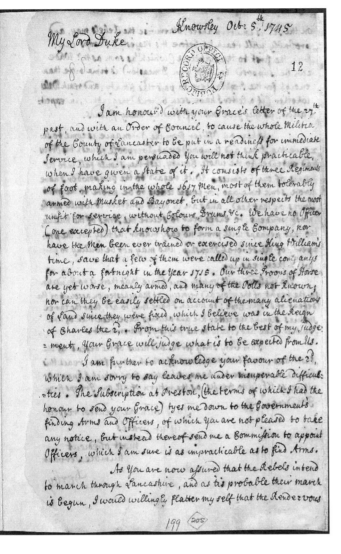

effectual.[50] Although Derby decided action must be taken, 'nothing in my power shall be wanting to preserve the peace of this county', he was unsure exactly what it should be. On 22 September, he thus decided to summon a meeting of the county elite.[51]

There was a meeting of nobility, gentry and clergy at Preston on 26 September to discuss methods of how to oppose the rebellion. Derby was despondent at the results, writing that he was 'sorry to tell your Grace the event has not answered our expectations'. This was in part because of the shocking news of Cope's defeat, which 'causes here the utmost consternation' and convinced many that the only adequate defence would be regular troops, who were a long way away.[52] However a newspaper reported the matter differently 'There never was a greater, or better, Spirit seen, even some who were suspected of different inclinations, expressed themselves very honestly and subscribed largely'.[53]

[Figure 8]
The Earl of Derby describes the county meeting at Preston in September 1745. Reproduced by permission of The National Archives. TNA, SP36/70, f208r.

Once the association method was decided upon, Newcastle gave the necessary permission and promised to find half-pay officers to train the men and to despatch sufficient arms for them.[54] Even so, there was a myriad of difficulties in forming this regiment. Firstly, there was a scarcity of half-pay officers.[55] Then there was the problem of Derby's health.[56] Finally there had been difficulties in raising funds. Derby thought some only subscribed 'only to save appearances'. Initially only £5,000 had been promised from those at the general meeting, though Derby hoped that by sending the subscription lists to other towns might increase it to £10,000.[57] Eventually, though, at least £11,000 was raised.[58]

It is not very clear who paid these subscriptions in Lancashire, as no list survives. Most sums which were collected in Lancashire were listed town by town, and were collected from door-to-door subscriptions. For example. Manchester contributed £1,879 and Rochdale, £1,300. Robert Patten claimed that some refused 'the property of those towns being much in the hands of Roman Catholics'.[59] Likewise, Hoghton noted that 'Mr Molyneux and the rest are so backward' in assisting with the raising of the militia.[60] Yet on the other hand, at the meeting at Ormskirk, 'every subscriber that was here present, was very unanimous and cheerful in their desires of paying the subscription'.[61]

A similar method was used in Cheshire, with warrants being sent to Cholmondeley on 21 September.[62] Yet, in Chester, the initial response at the county meeting was quite different, for opposition there seemed to be absent 'even the Catholics of the best distinction shew'd their zeal for the government'.[63] *The Westminster Journal* elaborated on this and provided a possible explanation that their support was a display of 'their Gratitude for the Peace they had long enjoyed under his [George II's] mild administration'.[64] This was noted by others: Henry Pelham (1694–1754), the First Lord of the Treasury (and Newcastle's brother), wrote 'they have had great favour shown from this government'.[65] As will be seen, the full weight of the penal laws was not implemented, perhaps because to have done so might have inflamed the situation and pushed Catholics over into rebellion.

There is partial information as to who paid these subscriptions. Sir Robert Grosvenor, MP, gave £2,000 to the Cheshire Association. The latter's action was surprising for he was a Tory whose family had Jacobite links. Most, though, gave smaller amounts, ranging from clergymen giving £2 2s to noblemen such as Cholmondeley with £300. All in all, £3,625 18s was raised at the first meeting, though the figure rose to an unknown level. Some also gave to similar Associations. Lonsdale gave £200 to the Yorkshire Association.[66] As for other subscribers, the parochial subscription of Downholland, Lancashire, is revealing; £25 being promised from the inhabitants. They were 32 in all and ascribed their names to a document. Presumably all were of humble rank. Of these, five were female and illiterate and three were illiterate males, which suggest that political consciousness existed even at a relatively humble level, and among women, too. Lancaster Quakers subscribed £150.[67]

By the end of October, however, some progress had been made. In Lancashire, the men 'likely young fellows' were variously uniformed in brown, blue, red and white cloth. Some were armed with muskets. Hoghton was making efforts to secure weapons for the rest of the men.[68] Parish constables endeavoured to assist. At Downholland, shooting butts were repaired and a watch bill and a musket repaired. The Aughton constable brought in the militia's arms. Gunpowder was purchased. Militia men were reimbursed by the Tarleton constable.[69] In Cumberland and Westmorland, constables also provided weapons and men for the militia. The Troutbeck

[Figure 9]
The walls and
gateway of Chester.
Photograph by the
author (2005).

constables supplied seven muskets, powder and swords, and made payments to the militia men.[70] Similar payments were made to the Firbank constables.[71] In Aughton, the constable claimed money for having kept watch on a number of occasions and a man was paid for bringing news of the Jacobites.[72]

Numbers enrolling into the militia forces varied. In Cumberland and Westmorland, 500 men made up the five companies of Militia Foot, and there were 69 men who made up the two troops of Militia Horse of those counties.[73] Each township provided a number of men for the infantry, whilst landowners supplied men and horses for the cavalry contingent.[74] The theoretical number in Lancashire was 1,624 men, including, possibly, three troops of cavalry.[75]

Although Cholmondeley had planned to raise the militia, this turned out to be impossible because the rolls of names of those who were obliged to supply men and horses was missing; nor were there any arms. Instead, he, along with another dozen noblemen, petitioned the King to be allowed to raise new regiments along the lines of the regular army. He was given permission to do so, but these newly raised levies were probably of limited military value. Despite the efforts of the 'disaffected', Cholmondeley raised 600 men by 8 November, 'a success I did not expect'.[76]

These militia and volunteers were not seen as a substitute for the regular troops, though in the past historians have condemned them for not acting in this role. As we have noted, the Lancashire Lieutenancy did not believe that their men would be able to act against the Jacobites, though Hoghton thought that they were in 'good order'. Despite this, Newcastle hoped that Derby's men might act in Lancashire in a manner that 'shall be most proper for that purpose; and for preserving the peace and tranquillity there'.[77] Hoghton agreed, stating 'We can keep our own county from rising but cant face the enemy except [if] some regular troops come this road'.[78]

A rather different role was envisaged for the more northerly forces. Initially the Militia of Cumberland and Westmorland were distributed in the towns of the two counties. However, they were marched into Carlisle in mid-October 1745, following a letter requesting the same from the acting governor of the city, Colonel Durand, to Lonsdale. It was thought that they were essential for the defence of the town and castle.[79] Similarly, Cholmondeley's regiment stood guard in Chester.[80]

The Lieutenancy in all the north-westerly counties had all raised forces from scratch, in one form or another, either by the traditional method of the militia, as in Cumberland and Westmorland, and, eventually, in Lancashire, or by means of forming a regiment of 'regulars', as in Cheshire. All, however, were scattered and their military prowess was, at best, limited. Yet none had been apathetic, and, despite doubts and despondency, all had done their best in support of George II.

The defence of Carlisle and Liverpool

Of all the places in the north west, it is Carlisle that has attracted most attention from historians of the Forty Five. Despite ultimate failure, the city's magistrates made preparations to defend the city. Pattinson, as Deputy Mayor, was in charge, though, unaccountably, Henry Aglionby was the mayor and resident in Carlisle. When Joseph Backhouse replaced him as mayor, Pattinson remained in charge throughout the crisis.[81] Pattinson's reputation has suffered much abuse. According to Waugh, his thoughts 'reached no further than securing his own property' and a hostile ballad claimed his horizons were limited to 'mouldy cheese and bacon grease'.[82]

[Figure 10] 'South or main entrance of Carlisle Castle and Drawbridge, in 1745', from *Carlisle in 1745: Authentic Account of the Occupation of Carlisle in 1745 by Prince Charles Edward Stuart.* Edited by George Gill Mounsey, 1846. Reproduced by permission of Carlisle Library.

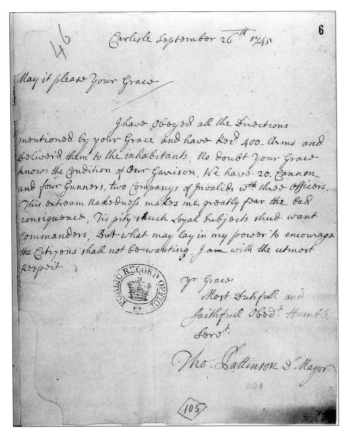

Carlisle September 26th 1745

6

May it please Your Grace

I have Obeyd all the Directions mentioned by your Grace and have Recd 400. Arms and delivered them to the inhabitants, No doubt Your Grace knows the condition of Our Garrison, We have 20. Cannon and four Gunners, two Companys of Invalids with three officers, This extream Nakedness makes me greatly fear the bad consequence, 'Tis pity such Loyal subjects shud want Commanders, But what may lay in my power to encourage the Citizens shall not be wanting, I am with the utmost Respect

yr Grace
Most Dutifull and faithfull Obedt Humble Servt.

Tho. Pattinson D Mayor

[Figure 11]
Thomas Pattinson describes the weaknesses of Carlisle's military defences in September 1745. Reproduced by permission of The National Archives. State Papers Domestic, 36/69, f105r.

Yet, with all attention focussed on the siege itself, the preparations in its wake have been unexamined by historians. In fact, Pattinson showed great foresight for he asked the government for arms to be sent up before Prestonpans; an order from London of 18 September refers to the despatch of 300 muskets and bayonets to Carlisle.[83] Throughout October, steps were taken for the defence of Carlisle. Newcastle sent Pattinson officers' commissions enabling him to raise men to form volunteer troops.[84] Soon afterwards, Pattinson had 400 muskets distributed to the inhabitants for the defence of the city. Yet he was not initially confident about his chances, writing 'what may lay in my power to encourage the citizens shall not be wanting'.[85] Lonsdale also acknowledged Pattinson's dilemma, writing 'He is in great Distress to know how to conduct himself, if the Rebels attack'.[86] Yet for all his understandable nervousness, Pattinson wrote on 2 October 'We are resolved to defend for His Majesty's Government and are not afraid of them, but could wish for some military assistance'.[87] This was not unreasonable; the military defence of the city and castle was in the hands of two weak companies of invalids, totalling 80 men and there were only four gunners to serve 20 guns.[88]

Newcastle passed on his thanks to Pattinson, but also told him that little military aid could be sent, as forces were concentrated in the north east. However, he did send orders on 3 October for Colonel Durand to command the garrison, in lieu of a resident governor or even a lieutenant governor.[89] Durand was described as 'a good officer and also a tolerable engineer', but without any complement of troops, his influence could only be limited.[90]

There was a great deal of activity in Carlisle. Pattinson had provisions from the neighbouring countryside gathered into the city to supply the castle.[91] On 30 September, the city minutes record that an order was made for 100 bushels of potatoes and 50 of oatmeal 'for the service of the city'.[92] Military stores were gathered from the countryside and cannons ordered from Whitehaven.[93] Strangers were stopped and examined and two suspects were arrested.[94] Recorder Richard Gilpin recorded that work on erecting earthworks for gun batteries had been completed. Deal boxes had been placed on the walls in order to keep the guns dry. Fires and candles were ready to be lit to help the guards at night time. Meanwhile, townsmen had volunteered for duty as guards and in helping to man the guns.[95]

The corporation had had to send messengers to raise the trained bands; six in all, indicating that some of the volunteers lived outside Carlisle. One of those making journeys towards raising men was Pattinson himself.[96] The 400 volunteers were divided into nine companies. Unfortunately they were untrained and undisciplined and so of limited military use. In fact, they were never even reviewed. This was because the men were reluctant to be taken away from their paid employments.[97]

The companies were probably officered each with one captain, one lieutenant and one ensign, as 27 commissions had to be written at the expense of £1 12s. 8d. in total.[98] Uniforms do not seem to have been worn, but hats were bought for three sergeants and coats for another three men. Although the men were armed with muskets, some swords and halberds were cleaned and mended.[99]

Other payments were made in order to assist with the defence. Coals and candles were bought in October and November to keep those standing guard warm during the night and to supply light in case of any intruders. Expense on candles was particularly high from 9 to 14 November, when the Jacobites were at the gates. There was also money spent on expenses entailed in making journeys about the county and for letters to Lonsdale and Newcastle.[100]

For all their efforts, the corporation had its faults. They were sometimes slow in acceding to Durand's requests. They were reluctant in walling up the Scotch and Irish gates as this 'would be an infinite prejudice to the city' presumably as regards trade. Likewise, when Durand suggested that they pull down buildings and sheds near to the city wall in order to give the guns a clearer arc of fire, they 'said it was private property, and that they would not do it'. Eventually, though, the gates were walled up and some property was pulled down.[101]

As long as the Jacobites stayed in Scotland, morale was high, as Pattinson told Newcastle on 7 October 'The loyal Corporation and Townsmen are in good heart'.[102] Ten days later, he reported 'as to this city we are not in the least afraid of the Rebels, being resolved to defend it to the utmost of our power'. Likewise on 28 October, Dorothy Palmer wrote 'nor do we think the Rebills will attempt to take Carlisle should they come this way, the place being well provided with all things for a siege, and the inhabitants resolved to loose their lives before they surrender'.[103]

Further to the south, there was a flurry of military activity on the part of the corporation of Liverpool. Even before the news of the debacle of

A VIEW *of* ANTIENT CARLISLE, *as represented in a Plate above* 100 *Years old.*

A The Caftle	H High ftreet	O The Citadell
B Caldoe gate, or the Irifh gate	I Bother gate, or Englifh gate	P Caftle orchard
C St Cuthberts	K Alnet well lane	Q The river *Eden*, and Stan-
D St Mary's	L Caftle gate ftreet	wick bridge
E The Shambles	M Fifhmarket	R The river *Cauda*
F The Mote hall	N Battail holme	
G Rickard gate, or the Scotch gate		

[Figure 12] 'A View of Antient CARLISLE, as represented in a Plate above 100 Years Old'. *The Gentleman's Magazine*, XV, 1745.

Prestonpans, Liverpool's corporation, as that of Carlisle, had decided to act, even without the presence of Owen Pritchard, the mayor, who was in Wales. His deputy, John Brooks, called a meeting on 20 September to discuss 'a proper method for securing this Town from any insult from the Rebells'. He and the town's principal citizens decided that a body of armed men should be raised and that an express be sent to the King to obtain his permission to do so, and for 'proper directions and assistance suitable'.[104]

A reply was received promptly. Newcastle told Brooks that the King 'extreamly approves the zeal and attention to his service, which you and the other magistrates of Liverpool have shew'd'. A warrant, bearing the King's sign manual, directed to the Mayor, authorising the formation of troops and the granting of commissions to those he thought fit to be officers, was sent on 23 September.[105]

It seems that about £6,000 was raised to finance the regiment. Of this sum, £2,000 was raised out of public stock and the remainder by the townspeople. According to a contemporary historian, James Ray, there was great enthusiasm among all ranks for such a project, 'the chearfulness and alacrity with which everyone contributed to the forwarding of this noble Design; since even the poorer sort did not refuse to case in their Mite, and the rich were not slack in giving according to their Abilities'.[106]

It was a fairly professional force. It eventually comprised eight companies of infantry, perhaps numbering 600–700 men in all. Although most of the officers were merchants and others with local social standing and wealth, but no military credentials, the men were led by regular officers, Colonels Graham and Gordon (the only half-pay officers despatched to the north west). These officers helped in the training of the men. They were uniformed in blue coats and were called the Liverpool Regiment of Blues. However, they were not armed until early November, when arms from the Tower were eventually dispatched northwards.[107]

Outside the auspices of public bodies, the Earl of Warrington encouraged his tenants to resist the Jacobites by promising them that if they enlisted against them and were killed on active service, he would add another life to the leases they held (leases of land were usually limited to a given number of lives).[108] He gave arms to his tenants for this purpose and they signed their names to a list of those ready to defend King George.[109]

Apart from purely military means, other steps were taken in these counties against the rebellion as it progressed in Scotland. Information was passed to the government from Scotland and elsewhere via various postmasters in the county. The first was from that of Lancaster on 24 September, relating news of the Jacobites in Scotland as collected by the Whigs of Dumfries.[110] News of Prestonpans was relayed by his opposite number in Preston on the following day.[111] Information from Scotland was also sent on by these men in the following month. [112]

Anti-Catholicism

There was also a need to combat the alleged danger inside the counties; the Catholics, whom some feared would assist the Jacobites. The Lords Lieutenant were ordered by the Privy Council on 5 September to pass orders to the Justices of the Peace (JPs) 'that they do, with the utmost Diligence, put the Laws in Execution against Papists, Reputed Papists and non jurors, being dangerous to His Majesty's Government, and that they tender to them the said Oaths and Declarations'. Failure for Catholics and others to do this meant that they would have their horses and arms seized and be confined to house arrest.[113] In the case of Cumberland, Lonsdale sent a letter to Thomas Simpson, clerk of the peace, and in the case of Westmorland, he wrote to the JPs, to tell them of these instructions and to bid them carry them out and transmit the details to him.[114]

Lonsdale was a little tardy in dealing with the orders concerning the Catholics, taking action only on 14 September. Again, he forwarded the orders in council to Simpson, which he was expected to copy and transmit to the JPs and the deputy lieutenants. Lonsdale also wrote directly to the JPs and deputies, instructing them to execute these instructions. The latter were told 'You must be so sensible of the great Importance of this Service in this Conjuncture that I cannot doubt of your Vigilance herein'. He expected, too, to be kept informed of any action taken.[115]

It is not certain how far such orders were carried out. Certainly the Westmorland order books do not make any reference to them whatsoever. Reading through these, one would not have thought that anything untoward occurred in the county in the years 1745 and 1746. There are references to poor relief, bastardy, the licensing of ale houses, bridges, common assault and other routine matters which were brought to the attention of the JPs each year.[116] Yet there is a scrap of paper among Lonsdale's correspondence which suggests otherwise. On 26 October, a list of Catholics of the two wards in the county was drawn up at Appleby and these people were summoned to take the oaths.[117] Yet activity on a countywide basis was clearly uneven, for parish accounts for Troutbeck and Firbank in Westmorland make no reference to expenditure on such.[118]

In Lancashire there seems to have been a reluctance to put

[Figure 13] Chester Cathedral. By the author (2005).

into practice the anti-Catholic laws and to have Catholic property searched for horses and arms. This was despite the county's most ardent magistrate wishing to do so. Hoghton complained that 'one who was to put it into execution has refused and the other has made excuses'.[119] Others disagreed with him, arguing that such steps would drive Catholics into the arms of the Jacobites rather than render them incapable of aiding them, and the Privy Council were of this opinion, too. Since Hoghton was not sent lists of the county's Catholics he could not act and so nothing was done against the Catholics.[120] The constable of Downholland made searches for suspected persons, perhaps including Catholics. He went with the High Constable to search Catholic properties for arms and horses. At Aughton, the constable's accounts record £1 1s 10d for expenses while 'making search for arms and horses'[121] Nor were there any such orders recorded in the archives of the Chester Quarter Sessions – this was clearly not a high priority here, either.

On the whole, despite orders from London, generally speaking, the magistrates either could not or would not act against the Catholics. Nowhere was the same severity applied as it had been in 1715.

The Anglican Clergy

The Anglican Church was also busy. The clergy, who outnumbered the civil magistrates, were seen as crucial in the defence of the status quo. Samuel Peploe (1668–1752) was bishop of Chester, and a fervent anti-Jacobite, having played a conspicuous part as vicar of Preston during the Fifteen. But Peploe was 77 in 1745 and could not act with the energy necessary for the task. Yet, despite his age, Peploe was far from being ineffective, as much as it lay within his limited power. He preached a sermon at Chester Cathedral on 13 October. Although at first he dwelt on general themes, claiming that the Jacobites would subvert religion, laws,

[Figure 14]
Plaque in Chester Cathedral commemorating Bishop Samuel Peploe's anti-Jacobite sermon in 1745. Photograph by the author (2005).

liberties and lives, he swiftly moved to his chief theme, which was anti-Catholic. He declared 'I may raise in your Minds a Just Detestation of Popery'. He discussed the backward nature of Catholicism, with idolatry, image worship, superstition, legends in an 'unknown' language (presumably Latin), addresses to saints and angels which led to other errors and lies. Who would want to change the 'Light of the Gospel for the

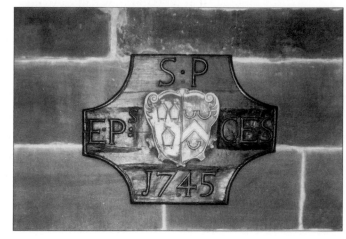

Darkness of Popery?' he rhetorically asked. Peploe also referred to the allegedly secular impact of Catholic rule. 'Nor are their horrid Cruelties less known. What Blood have the Papists not spilt?' He ended by trusting his congregation would not be deluded by fair promises, but that they would count their current blessings and not endanger them from France and the Pope. Finally he trusted that God would protect Britain as God had done in ages past.[122]

Peploe was not entirely inactive in other ways, either. He attended the meeting of the county gentry at Chester on 2 October and subscribed £200 to the loyalist association – the same sum that the Archbishop of York was to subscribe to the Yorkshire Association, though the archbishopric's income was four times that of Chester.[123] He also asked his friends in Manchester to keep local Jacobites under strict observation, and to persuade others that a successful invasion would mean Popery, French domination and commercial ruin and, as for the Whigs, attempted 'to keep up their good inclinations'.[124]

Sir George Fleming (1667–1747), bishop of Carlisle, was also elderly. Mounsey observed, 'his advanced age, of seventy eight years' precluded him from any very active exercise'.[125] Likewise, Waugh noted in 1747 that Fleming had 'been long in a declining way'.[126] Waugh was somewhat critical, though probably not unfairly, about his superior. Fleming appears to have been content to leave matters in the hands of others, especially his vigorous Chancellor. When the matter of a county meeting of gentry and clergy was mentioned, Waugh wrote that he would:

> hint it to our Bishop, but I doubt he is so timorous he will propose nothing; however, I now hear from him, or see him everyday, and am his dear Chancellor, he is so pleased with my intelligence. My Lord Bishop has been with me; I have mentioned this thing to him, he has not resolved, but will wait my answer from Sir James Lowther, and if he approves it, would have me go to the meeting.[127]

Yet Fleming was not always absent from such gatherings. He attended a meeting at Carlisle in late October when it appeared that the militia might have to disband as their month's service was at an end. Apparently, 'The Bishop said everything he could to engage them to keep up the Militia and had great influence upon them'.[128]

Fleming's name was appended to the loyal addresses sent by the counties of both Cumberland and Westmorland in late October 1745.[129] Yet it was Waugh who composed this 'as the bishop could not attend the meetings, I was obliged to do it in his name'.[130] Fleming seems to have spent most of the period of the crisis at his palace, Rose Castle. On 8 September, he addressed Humphrey Senhouse thus 'The Disturbance in the Highlands seem daily to increase…should they move this way, which God forbid, we should be tempted to fly to your country for a Retreat'.[131] Six days later, he had had no further news of the rebellion, but added 'God grant this storm may blow over without any bad consequences'.[132]

Although not the most senior clergyman in the region, it is Waugh who emerges as the most dynamic in the north west. In 1747 he boasted to Newcastle of his woes during the crisis, namely 'the losses I sustained, the fatigues I underwent and the expenses I was put to were very great'.[133] As already noted, he certainly appears to have been farsighted. In August, at a meeting of magistrates of both Cumberland and the Lowlands of Scotland to discuss issues relating to turnpike roads, Waugh entered into an agreement with his northern colleagues that they exchange information about the Jacobites if the need arose.[134]

Even though he was alarmed and concerned at the parlous state of defences in Carlisle, Waugh acted his part in the intelligence network as planned.[135] He kept up a correspondence from September to November about Jacobite activity in Scotland, writing chiefly to Newcastle. He acted as a conduit from loyalist Scots and passed their information to London. Chief among his informants was the Whig mayor of Dumfries. The first letter was forwarded on 14 September. These letters included a 'Melancholy Account' of Prestonpans, of contributions demanded from Glasgow, movements of the Jacobite army and information from Edinburgh.[136] Yet, with the arrival of that army in England, the supply of information was disrupted and he admitted on 7 November 'Nothing that can be depended upon with the least degree of certainty has come to my knowledge since…yesterday' as informants had fled.[137] Yet he was not dismayed. On the eve of the Jacobite army's arrival near Carlisle, 9 November, he wrote 'I have been up most part of the night settling the Dispatches and doing other Duty'.[138]

Waugh was also active locally. In September, he declared 'I flatter myself I have been of no small use since I have not wasted inclination nor industry'.[139] When Durand arrived on 11 October, Waugh wrote that 'every civility and all the assistance in the power of me, or my friends, will be most cheerfully and readily offered to him'.[140] Waugh's actions were certainly appreciated in London. Newcastle wrote on 19 September 'His Majesty received, in the most gracious manner, the seasonable mark of the loyalty and zeal, which you and the rest of these gentlemen, have shewn'.[141]

The junior clergy also acted against the Jacobites. Some clergymen gave generously to pay towards the county forces; one gave £400.[142] Although they seem to have had little encouragement from their masters, some in Lancashire certainly acted in favour of the status quo and followed Peploe's lead. Elizabeth Byrom (1722–1801) of Manchester noted in her diary that the Manchester clergy did so in early October 1745. According to her, Mr. Joseph Hoole (d.1745), the Rector of St. Ann's, Thomas Lewthwaite, Assistant Curate and Benjamin Nicholls, Vicar of Eaton, all preached against the Jacobites. Indeed, copies of one of Nicholls' sermons was published and sold at six pence each. Elsewhere in Lancashire, Dr. James Fenton (1688–1767), Vicar of Lancaster, preached against the Jacobites.[143]

Following Waugh's lead, the other members of Carlisle cathedral's chapter signed a loyal association pledging their support to George II.[144] Some took duty in watching out for the enemy with their spy glasses on the tower of the Cathedral. Others took up arms as volunteers and acted as messengers and ADCs to Durand 'with a coolness and resolution that became them'.[145] As noted above, clergy also subscribed to the Cheshire Association and, as already mentioned, attended the county meetings at Chester and Preston.

The only published sermon which has survived from this period, except that of Peploe's, is that of the Rev. Thomas Maddox (1713–1783) of Liverpool, who preached on 29 September 1745, and this was later printed at the behest of the corporation. He claimed that he had 'an Heart warm'd with true zeal for our happy constitution, both in Church and State'.[146] He compared Britain's plight to that of the Israelites against the Ammomites, and then went on to list the reasons why a stand against the Jacobites should be made. These sentiments, which were similar to those made by other clergymen throughout England, were as follows: the Jacobites were backed by France and were Catholic. All the usual anti-Catholic arguments were brought out – that they were responsible for 'inhuman Cruelties' in the past and had 'barbarous and bloody principles'. Positively, the blessings of the status quo, namely, peace and prosperity under a mild and prudent administration, were played up. What was required was sincere repentance to regain God's blessing and to present a united opposition against the Jacobites.[147] Unfortunately, there are no surviving sermons of clergymen from Cumberland and Westmorland; probably because none were published, such was the scarcity of printing presses in these counties, compared to those to the south.

There were also loyalist actions taken in the parish churches throughout the counties. This took the form of ringing the bells to mark loyalist anniversaries, such as the King's birthday, the anniversary of his Coronation and 5 November, a red letter day for Protestants marking both the discovery of the Gunpowder Plot in 1605 and the arrival of William of Orange in Torbay in 1688. At Ribchester, the bell ringers were paid 11 shillings to ring on 5 November. Similar celebrations occurred at Padiham, Maghull and Kirkham. At Downholland, there was a bonfire on this day.[148]

As with those parishes in Lancashire, those in Westmorland and Cumberland rang their church bells on loyalist occasions. The parish of Beetham also rang on 5 November 1745.[149] The parish of Heversham celebrated the King's birthday and on 5 November.[150] The ringing of church bells reminded all those within earshot of the loyalties of those ordering the bell ringing. Churches in Cumberland also seemed unanimously loyalist. However, such expenditure represented an additional burden on poorer parishes.

Some clergy were less active. Rev. George Williamson (1706–1783), Curate of Arthuret in Cumberland, kept a diary and his laconic comments are not indicative of great zeal at this period. He records rumours and facts; including the fall of Edinburgh and the battle of Prestonpans, among his references to fishing and hunting. But there are no personal comments or feelings recorded here, nor any evidence of making sermons against the Jacobites or anything about activity by his brother clergymen. Whether this is because of the lack of activity, or whether he simply did not mention it, is impossible to discern.[151]

Fear and loyalism

The responses of the inhabitants were polarised. There was a great deal of fear among many. In early October, it was noted that 'Days of Humiliation and prayers are appointed in several Dissenting Congregations'.[152] Manchester Presbyterians were fearful and so 'sent everything that's valuable away, wives, children, and all, for fear of the rebels'.[153] They were not alone in this; in late September, the ardent loyalist, Hoghton, wrote of 'securing our Plate, Writings & Effects the best way we can'.[154] Likewise, in Cumberland; Sir John Pennington reported on 23 September, 'I hear Sir Philip Musgrave's family are gone for London this Day and several other families are removing out of this county'.[155] It is possible that some of this panic may have been the result of the all too successful dissemination of propaganda. Country people had 'been assured from Creditable people that the highlanders were a Savage Sett of people and eat all the young Children'.[156]

Such propaganda included sermons, but also secular publications, too. The principal local organ was *The Manchester Magazine*. Verse and prose which had been published elsewhere was printed here. In one issue an address by the Bishop of Worcester was published, speaking out against the Catholics and French allies of the Jacobites and of the benefits of the status quo. There was also 'A Calm Address', aimed at all parties in religion, especially the Catholics, which stressed the fact that an invasion by the French and Scots should alarm all, even if they were not Protestants. Verses included 'A Faithful Soldier's Address' which contained terms such as 'Most Gracious George' and 'the Popish Brat'. Another anti-Catholic piece was 'The Danger of the Protestant Religion', which featured an account of the reign of James II. A report of a pope-burning ceremony at Deptford, Kent, was also published.[157]

There were other displays of public loyalty towards George II. In Manchester, often portrayed as a hotbed of Jacobitism, his birthday was celebrated by a bonfire being lit in his honour, and six days later, the anti-

Catholic day of remembrance, 5 November, was also marked in this way.[158] Similarly in Preston; the King's birthday was 'ushered in with Ringing of Bells'. Young men, allegedly eager to fight the would-be invader, paraded the streets with drums and colours 'amidst the loud acclamations of several thousands of people crying God save King George'. There were loyal toasts at The White Horse.[159] At Lancaster sentiments were the same, 'The People here seem very loyal and believe will do all in their power to oppose the Rebels, should they come this way'.[160] Likewise, on 30 October, George II's birthday, there is a reference in the Chamberlains' accounts for Carlisle 'Drink for four rejoicing days £2 13s. 4d.'[161] Ale was purchased for the commonalty presumably, on 11 October, on the anniversary of the King's Coronation.[162]

The reaction of the corporations at the onset of the crisis was to send loyal addresses to George II to stress their loyalty and abhorrence of the Jacobites. Almost every other corporation in the country did so, and the addresses are very much stereotyped and formulaic. How much they meant in any practical terms is debatable. In the previous year, in which there had been a flurry of such addresses in the wake of an attempted invasion from France, Horace Walpole (1717–1797), man of letters and a son of the recently deceased chief minister, had claimed, 'Addresses are come from all parts; but you know how little they are to be depended on – King James [II] had them.'[163] Not to have sent them, though, would have been viewed as being sympathetic towards the Jacobites.

The corporations of Lancaster and Liverpool were the first in the north west to send addresses, reaching the court in late September.[164] Chester's was close on its heels, in early October.[165] The address of Carlisle did not arrive until the end of the month.[166] Although these addresses were often stereotypical, corporations also used them to explicitly promote themselves. The address sent by Carlisle included the following words:

> in being honoured with your Royal mandate for arming ourselves against the Disturbers of your Majesty's Reign. And we hope, should the publick enemy approach us, that this important trust will not have been bestowed in vain, but that it will enable us to give a surer proof than words convey, of our firm attachment to your Majesty's Interest.[167]

Yet as September turned to October and there had been no onslaught from the north, panic subsided. Richard Kay, for instance, does not mention the Jacobites at all in his diary in October. It was not until 21 November, after the Jacobites had taken Carlisle, that he noted their progress again.[168] Even the despondent Derby noted on 22 October 'there seems in general to be an honest spirit among His Majesty's Protestant

St. James's, October 26.

THE following Addreſs of the Biſhop of Carliſle, Deputy Lieutenants, Juſtices of the Peace, Gentlemen, Clergy and Freeholders of the County of Weſtmorland, having been tranſmitted by the Right Honourable the Lord Viſcount Lonſdale, Lord Lieutenant of the ſaid County, to his Grace the Duke of Newcaſtle, one of his Majeſty's Principal Secretaries of State, has by him been preſented to his Majeſty: Which Addreſs his Majeſty was pleaſed to receive very graciouſly.

To the King's moſt Excellent Majeſty,

The humble Addreſs of ʻthe Biſhop of Carliſle, the Deputy Lieutenants, Juſtices of the Peace, Gentlemen, Clergy and Freeholders of the County of Weſtmorland.

May it pleaſe your Majeſty,

WE your Majeſty's moſt dutiful and loyal Subjects, the Lord Biſhop of Carliſle, the Deputy Lieutenants, Juſtices of the Peace, Gentlemen, Clergy and Freeholders of the County of Weſtmorland, humbly beg Leave to approach your Royal Throne, with Hearts full of the warmeſt Gratitude and Joy for your moſt ſeaſonable and ſafe Return to theſe Dominions. With equal Ardour and Sincerity we offer our Congratulations on the Succeſs of your Majeſty's Arms in the Reduction of Cape Breton, a Conqueſt not leſs glorious than important to us; and on the happy Event, which, under God, your Majeſty's conſummate Prudence and continual Labours to reſtore the Liberty and Tranquillity of Europe have produced, in placing the Imperial Crown upon the Head of one, who, we have the ſtrongeſt Reaſons to believe, will be both able and inclinable to eſtabliſh ſuch a Ballance of Power as may ſufficiently defend the Allies from all the Inſults of the common Enemy.

A deep Senſe of the many Bleſſings we enjoy under your Majeſty's juſt, mild, and gracious Government, obliges us to expreſs our utter Deteſtation and Abhorrence of each wicked Effort to deprive us of them; particularly of the preſent abſurd and unnatural Attempt to impoſe on us a Foreign, Popiſh, frequently abjured Pretender, to the Crown of theſe Realms.

On this extraordinary Occaſion we moſt humbly intreat your Majeſty to accept our freſh Aſſurances of Duty and unſhaken Loyalty; our ſolemn Engagements of endeavouring faithfully, in our reſpective Stations, to exert our utmoſt Zeal for the Protection of your Majeſty's moſt ſacred Perſon, the Support of your Government, the Preſervation of our happy Conſtitution in Church and State. And we ſhall not fail to implore the Divine Favour to continue theſe invaluable Bleſſings to us, thro' the Proſperity of your illuſtrious Houſe, in which we firmly truſt they are included, and thereby perpetuate the ſame to our Poſterity.

[Figure 15]
The Loyal Address of the County of Westmorland, October 1745. The wording of other addresses is very similar. *The London Gazette*, 8478, 22–26 October 1745.

subjects here'.[169] At Preston on 4 October, it was noted 'We are Quiet here and keep a Guard of 100 men every night of our Town's Men'.[170]

Soldiers were rarely popular in eighteenth century England, but it was reported in early October, of Cholmondeley's regiment of regulars, 'In every village he march'd thro' he was received with the warmest Acclamations'. In Warrington, soldiers were welcomed into private houses and in Manchester, 'a General Joy appeared in every Countenance'.[171] Fear of the Jacobites was clearly paramount over fears of the military.

Conclusion

From late September 1745, the authorities and people of the north-western counties were concerned, both by the Jacobite army in Scotland which might march southwards as well as any internal insurrection by the

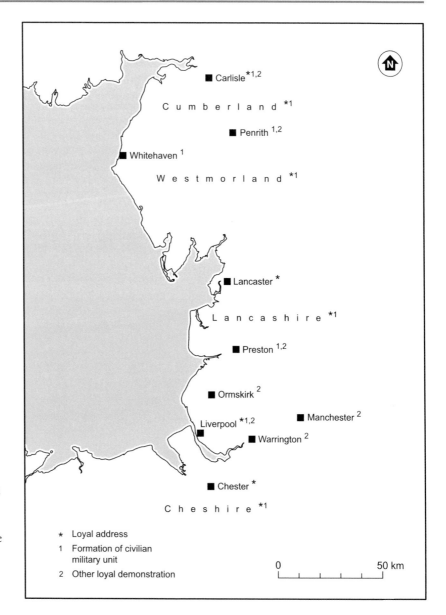

Carlisle[*1,2]

C u m b e r l a n d [*1]

Penrith [1,2]

Whitehaven [1]

W e s t m o r l a n d [*1]

Lancaster [*]

L a n c a s h i r e [*1]

Preston [1,2]

Ormskirk [2]

Manchester [2]

Liverpool [*1,2]

Warrington [2]

Chester [*]

C h e s h i r e [*1]

*   Loyal address
1   Formation of civilian
      military unit
2   Other loyal demonstration

0   50 km

[Map 2]
Map of the North
West of England
showing loyalties
towards the House
of Hanover, 1745.
Map drawn by
Simon Chew.

Catholics and others. Yet in the seven-week breathing space given to them, they had achieved much, starting on a base of almost nothing. Carlisle's defences had been strengthened, stores gathered together, and the county militia drawn within, together with the volunteers raised by the town. In Lancashire, Liverpool and Cheshire, forces had been raised, too. Little, though, had been done about the Catholics, who some believed to be potential traitors. The Anglican Church had also been active in promoting loyalty to King George, as had the local press, and there had been other demonstrations of pro-Hanoverian loyalty. So much for those historians who argue that the north west was lukewarm towards the existing dynasty or that they were cautious time servers, waiting to see which side won before venturing any strong opinions or actions. Jacobite responses had been muted. Yet all these gestures by loyalists were perhaps inadequate. These counties were, after all, unguarded by regular troops and were therefore still open to invasion.

CHAPTER TWO

The Jacobite Invasion of England: November 1745

At the end of October, unbeknown to anyone in England, the Jacobite high command in Edinburgh met to discuss the army's next move. By now it had grown considerably, numbering about 5,500 men. In many ways it resembled a regular army, with 13 variously sized infantry battalions, armed with muskets and swords, six small cavalry units and 13 cannons. It was paid regularly by means of the appropriation of 'public money', taxes ordinarily collected for George II's government. Yet, on 30 October, its command now faced a major decision. Money was becoming scarce and Field Marshal Wade, with a substantial army of regulars, had reached Newcastle upon Tyne and it was probable that this army would march northwards to confront the Jacobites.

There were two decisions to be made. Firstly, should the Jacobites invade England, as Scots armies had done in 1640, 1648, 1651 and 1715, which, save for the first, had all been unsuccessful? Or should they remain in Scotland and fight there? It was decided by the narrowest of margins (one vote) to take the initiative and invade England. Secondly, which route into England should the force take? Charles was in favour of the north-eastern route, which had been used in 1640. This would mean fighting Wade's troops almost at once, but this force – believed to be weak with sickness after a sea voyage or exhausted by long marches and low in morale – should not, it was thought, present too difficult a challenge. One of his lieutenant generals, Lord George Murray, preferred the traditional north-western route via Carlisle, in order to avoid a military decision until more support could be raised. It was this option which gained most favour. The army left Edinburgh in two columns by 4 November, with one column feinting towards the north east to keep Wade at Newcastle. Both columns joined before Carlisle on 9 November.[1]

It is important to realise that the Jacobites expected a great deal of support in England, yet only one agent had been despatched prior to the invasion to rouse them. In late September, one Hickson, a Perth vintner, went to Newcastle in order to raise the northern Jacobites. The dramatic message he carried from Charles included the immortal line 'they [the English Jacobites] will be inexcusable before God and man, if they do not do all in their power to assist and support me in such an undertaking'. They were to join him as

soon as he crossed into England and to supply money and provisions. However, Hickson was soon captured and sent to London.[2] No other contacts had been made, nor were attempted as far as is known. Apart from the Jacobite Chevalier de Johnstone's assertion below, there is no evidence that any English Jacobites sent messages to Charles (as southern Jacobites had in 1743). This was an inauspicious start to the invasion of England.

[Figure 16]
Edinburgh Castle. The only part of the city never to be taken by the Jacobites
Photograph by the author (2005).

Both Charles and Murray had spoken of support from England. Charles had thought that a victory over Wade would give his friends in Lancashire, Yorkshire and elsewhere the chance to join him. Murray believed that a march to Carlisle would enable Jacobites in Northumberland and Lancashire to enlist (overlooking the problems of geography for Lancashire Jacobites). Charles certainly seems to have believed that they would be met in their march through northern England by his supporters. Another senior Jacobite officer, Lord Elcho, claimed Charles said 'he was sure all the Country [England] would join him'.[3] Johnstone wrote 'he [Charles] had received letters from several English lords, assuring him that he should find them in arms on the borders ready to join him with a considerable English force.'[4] These promises were probably made in order to overcome the reluctance of many Scots chiefs to leave Scotland and invade England.[5]

Although any support given by the English Jacobites would probably have been militarily insignificant (poorly armed and untrained men led by amateurs as they would have been), it was nonetheless crucial. The reluctance of many of the Scots to leave their native soil had been largely overcome by promises of English support. According to Johnstone 'Some of the chiefs even told him, that they had taken arms, and risked their fortunes and their lives, to seat him [Charles] on the throne of Scotland, but they wanted nothing to do with England' but that Charles assured them of substantial English support, and so 'the chiefs of the clans suffered themselves at length to yield and, after many debates, gave their assent to his proposition'. Likewise, Elcho recalled 'The Common people were quite averse to Going to England' and needed similar assurances about English and French support.[6] It was psychologically vital, therefore, that the Jacobite army was joined by numerous English supporters, especially men of high social position. Military victory in England over one of the regular armies or a French invasion might tip the balance and result in large scale support as the cause looked like being successful, as might a collapse of the regime. The invasion of England, therefore, represented a gamble, not only militarily but of Charles' personal credibility, and one of the key determinants would be whether there was substantial support from the heartland of Hanoverian Britain. The responses towards the Jacobite army

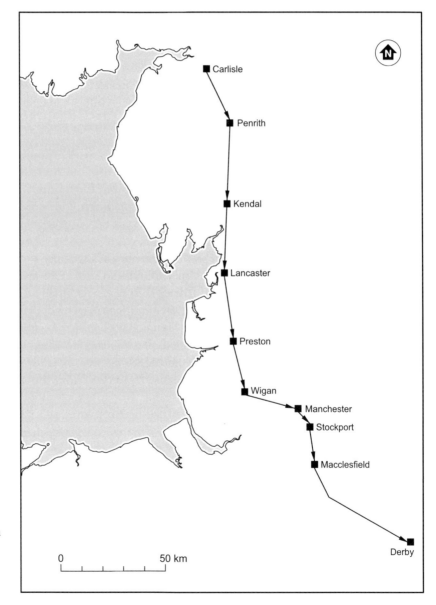

[Map 3]
Map showing the Jacobite advance through the North West of England in November 1745. Map drawn by Simon Chew.

on the route of march; ie. in the north west of England, would be an important determinant of the success of the invasion.

This chapter is divided into three sections, in order to consider responses in the counties as the Jacobite army marched south. It is not in strict chronological order, as all responses in each jurisdiction are assessed in that section. Thus, it discusses the counties in the order that the Jacobite army marched through them.

Cumberland and Westmorland

The Jacobite army crossed the River Esk and into England on 8 November and encamped at Brampton, a few miles east of Carlisle. Here, attempts were made to contact the English Jacobites. Henry Salkeld, an elderly Catholic gentleman, sent a messenger to Francis Strickland, one of Charles' supporters, 'to know whether his services would be agreeable as in that case he would join the Prince'. It was decided that, since the weather was cold, they did not require Salkeld's services. He was, however, later seen with the Jacobites in Carlisle.[7]

Yet it appears that Salkeld sent a former servant of his, Peter Pattinson, a Catholic grocer from Cumberland, who arrived at Brampton on 11 November. He was given a message from Thomas Sheridan, one of Charles' confidants, to England's foremost Jacobite peer, Barrymore. It told of the Jacobite army's successes to date and that their taking Carlisle was imminent. It stated that a march to London would then be taken. They optimistically hoped that they would be in Cheshire by 24 November and the letter ended with 'I hope you with all your friends in that county will be ready to join us. For now is the time or never'.[8]

Pattinson played his part. He departed for Cheshire on 14 November and went via Kendal, where he was joined by Thomas Newby. They arrived at Barrymore's Cheshire seat on 16 November. Yet the elderly peer was away in London, attending Parliament, which Charles had expressly forbidden his supporters to do, and the note was given to Lord Buttevant, Barrymore's son. When Buttevant read it and noted the sender, he was 'in a passion' and threw it into the fire. On the following day he had Pattinson and Newby arrested.[9] Yet even had Barrymore been at home, it is impossible to know what he would have done on receipt of the latter. John Murray later claimed that Barrymore, along with the other leading English Jacobites, 'would not do anything unless a sufficient Body of Troops were landed from France'.[10]

Encouraging signs for Charles were few in number. Most Catholic families put on a show of indifference. The only exception was at Warwick Hall, Brampton, for although the menfolk kept themselves aloof from the Jacobites, Mrs. Warwick, whose ancestors had fought for Charles I, apparently welcomed Charles and declared 'May God bless him'.[11]

[Figure 17]
Home of reluctant Jacobites: 'A View of Warwick-Hall in Cumberland on the River Eden'. To Francis Warwick Esq. of Warwick Hall. This plate is inscrib'd by his most obliged humble servant. William Bellers pinxit, G. Bickham, sculpsit. Published 17th January 1774. Reproduced by permission of Carlisle Library.

However, at the other extreme, panic had gripped some of the English. According to Elcho 'The people in England seemed mighty afraid of the army and had abandon'd all the villages upon its approach'.[12] On one occasion, Charles and his entourage stayed in an unspecified 'little house'. Whilst there, they found a little girl hiding under a bed and her mother:

called out for God's sake to Spare her Child, for She was the only remaining one of Seven she had bore. Upon which some of the gentlemen being curious to know what she meant, followed to the door and enquired what made her express herself in that manner. To which she answered that indeed She had been assured from Creditable people that the highlanders were a Savage Sett of people and eat all the young Children.[13]

According to Colonel O'Sullivan, a Jacobite officer, the people of the house were Quakers (usually hostile towards Jacobites). He recorded that once the woman had been assured that her baby was safe, other Quakers brought them good quality beer. One told Charles 'Thou are not a man, but an angel'.[14]

The official reaction in the county was hostile, as was soon learnt after Charles sent a message on 10 November, to the mayor of Carlisle, demanding he surrender the town.[15] As might have been expected from Pattinson's earlier behaviour, no answer was sent, except cannon fire. Much to the relief of the inhabitants of Carlisle, the Jacobite forces then moved away from the city to meet the threat of Wade's army, who, it was believed, was marching from Newcastle to the city's defence, and some hoped that Carlisle had seen off the attackers. Unfortunately for his reputation, Pattinson was among

[Figure 18]
The main gateway
of Carlisle Castle.
Photograph by
author (2004).

them. He wrote to the court, believing his defence to have been successful, and included the following comment 'And so I think the town of Carlisle has done His Majesty more service than the great city of Edinburgh, or all Scotland together'. For a very brief spell, Pattinson enjoyed an unmerited fame in London, having put the capital in 'great spirits'.[16] Lord Carlisle wrote 'The Mayor was in great credit here for a few days'.[17]

Two days later, when it was clear that the Jacobites had not retreated (Wade did not begin to march until 16 November and was soon forced to turn back) and were returning to take the city, there was, at first, apparent resolution as 'the Besieged all the time kept a Constant fire of Cannon & Small arms', though with little effect. Then panic arose. Threats were made by the Jacobites to scale the walls, and their trenches, dug by local men, apparently coerced into the task, were certainly close to the city walls – within musket shot in fact.[18] Some inhabitants feared they would be put to the sword if they resisted. After all, Charles' initial message included the ominous phrase 'the fatal Consequences which usually attend a Town's being taken by Assault'.[19] Pattinson asked Durand, as chief military officer, what they should do. Durand replied that they should make a stand. Pattinson agreed. He then held a meeting of the townsmen and there was, initially, a majority in favour of defending the town. The clergy went with others to the castle in hope of making a defence there.[20]

Yet the county militia officers wished to surrender. They were very dispirited and with good reason. During the siege, they and their men were

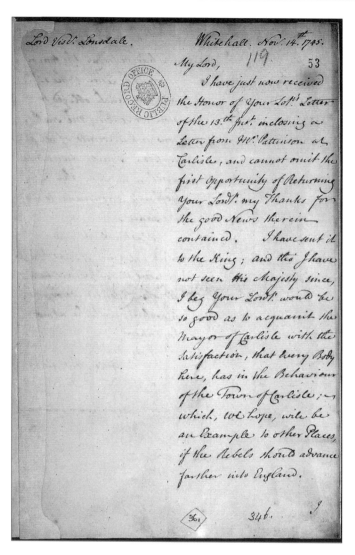

Lord Visct. Lonsdale.   Whitehall. Nov. 14th. 1745.

My Lord,   119   53

I have just now received the Honor of your Lordsp's Letter of the 13th. first. inclosing a Letter from Mr. Pattinson at Carlisle, and cannot omit the first opportunity of Returning your Lordsp. my Thanks for the good News therein contained. I have sent it to the King; and tho' I have not seen His Majesty since, I beg your Lordsp. would be so good as to acquaint the Mayor of Carlisle with the satisfaction, that every Body here, has in the Behaviour of the Town of Carlisle; — which, we hope, will be an Example to other Places, if the Rebels should advance farther into England.

'so sick by this Great fatigue'. They had not been relieved by the townsmen for a whole week.[21] Furthermore, Wade's forces were unable to relieve them. William Fletcher wrote on 17 November that 'the Militia proposed to keep the Rebels out 8 or 10 days longer if any promise of assistance in that time' had been given. However, Wade's message that he was unable to do so, but wished the defenders 'all imaginable success' had signalled the end of their hopes.[22]

Men began to leave their posts 'multitudes of them deserting every hour from the walls till the officers of many companies were at last left with not above three or four men'. Therefore, the officers claimed there was no option but to surrender.[23] This was a near unanimous decision; 18 officers voted in favour, three against and three were absent.[24] Some blamed them for the fall of the city. Waugh wrote 'Most of the militia officers came to our defence with great reluctance and stayed there from the first with us with great unwillingness'.[25] Pattinson agreed with Waugh, believing their behaviour unreasonable, adding that most of the townsmen wished to fight on.[26]

At first, the city magistracy had agreed merely to surrender the city conditionally, without agreeing to have the castle fall, by claiming to have no jurisdiction over the latter. Pattinson, Backhouse and 13 others voted against surrender, but were defeated by 24 who wished to surrender, including Gilpin and Waugh. The Jacobites wished both city and castle to surrender. After much bargaining with the Jacobite leaders, the magistrates capitulated. Pattinson and the aldermen were obliged to come to Charles at Brampton and to surrender the keys to the city, which they did on 15 November.[27]

Pattinson now became a figure of contempt, as Charles Robinson commented to Waugh, 'Everybody condemns the vanity of the Mayor in his letter to my Lord Duke of Newcastle'.[28] Much fun was had at Pattinson's expense. Believing himself safe in London, Horace Walpole wrote, with the wisdom of hindsight, after noting Pattinson's letter of triumph, 'But alack! The next day the Rebels returned...The great Mr Pattinson...instantly surrendered the town and agreed to pay two thousand pounds to save it from pillage. Well! Then we were assured that the citadel could hold out seven or eight days; but did not so many hours.'[29] Others were more understanding: Hoghton had written on 14 November 'I am afraid Carlisle will not hold out a great while, as there are such crowds of the rebels...and especially as the city expects no relief from Marshal Wade'.[30]

Not only did the magistracy have to offer the keys to Charles on their knees, but they were also obliged to proclaim his father as King James III and to read his manifesto at the market cross.[31] There is a reference to wine being drunk at The Bush public house in Carlisle for the Jacobite Duke of Perth's entourage when the capitulation was signed; whilst Pattinson and his colleagues spent £1 for wine for themselves.[32] Yet it is difficult to see what else could have been done. Lacking any relief from the regulars, a civilian garrison, outnumbered more than ten to one, had limited options. With the unwillingness of the militia to fight, Carlisle could not be held for want of manpower and so surrender was inevitable. As we shall see, when the Jacobite garrison of Carlisle was faced with overwhelming numbers and an imminent assault a few weeks later, they acted likewise. There is also evidence to suggest that Backhouse and James Pearson, the town clerk, were forced into making the proclamation mentioned above. Backhouse, though threatened, refused and Pearson, on pain of military execution, repeated words which were dictated to him, after claiming he did not know how to proclaim a king.[33] However, clergy who remained at Carlisle, such as Thomas Birkett (1707–1782), a prebendary and Robert Wardale (1706–1773), curate of Stanwix, were thought to have become rather friendly with the new governor, John Hamilton, though they claimed they remained to look after the Church's interests in the city.[34]

Waugh remained in Carlisle after the town surrendered, but not for long. On being asked to have prayers omitting the King's name read in the churches of Carlisle, he remarked 'I absolutely refused and hope no such irregularity either has or ever will be committed at Carlisle'.[35] He left the city two days later, his usefulness there limited, and went to Yorkshire.[36]

Despite the surrender, the populace seem to have been unenthusiastic about the Jacobites. Elcho recorded 'All the People both of that town and county shew'd a great dislike to the Prince's Cause'.[37] But they were not actively hostile, as James Maxwell, another Jacobite officer, records, 'The people of Carlisle seemed generally disaffected, but all expressed their sense of the great civility and amity with which they had been treated'.[38] Yet one Alexander Blair, wrote that Charles was greeted by 'the loudest acclamations you can imagine'.[39]

The impact of the fall of Carlisle was to dishearten the residents of Whitehaven. They had erected batteries and formed a garrison to defend the place against the Jacobites. They also intended to send men and military supplies to Carlisle. Yet after receiving news of Carlisle's fate, they took their cannon and military stores and loaded them upon boats in the harbour in case they fell into Jacobite hands.[40] Residents removed their goods on board ships to Dublin and the Isle of Man. An old woman carried away a large basket of empty bottles, 'rather than trust them to their Highland Civility'.[41]

They were not alone in their concern for their valuables. Some churches hid their plate on the Jacobite approach. Heversham in Westmorland spent a shilling 'when the church plate was hid'.[42] Likewise, at Greystoke, plate was hidden on several occasions 'when the Rebels came out of Scotland'.[43] Some clergy fled. The Rev. Thomas Symonds (1711–1789), Rector of Kendal, certainly did so, on hearing the news that the Jacobites were arriving.[44]

The fall of Carlisle may appear to have been an unqualified success for the Jacobites, but it was not. What was important was what had not happened. There had been no accrual of support towards their cause whatsoever. Indeed, on 18 November, there was discussion as to what to do next; whether they should remain in the vicinity of Carlisle, awaiting expected support, or to press on towards Lancashire. The latter was decided upon. In any case, funds were limited so movement was imperative.[45] Charles' optimism was undaunted, remarking 'he was sure all his English friends would join him in Lancashire'.[46] Johnstone recalled that the earlier promise of support on the borders had failed to materialise, but Charles claimed 'he had received fresh letters from his friends in England, assuring him that he should find all of them in arms, on his arrival at Preston'.[47] The army marched south, with its first elements leaving Carlisle on 20 November.

There was less terror caused by the Jacobite army at Penrith, presumably because the atrocity stories had not been backed up by reality. Yet as Elcho recorded 'At Penrith they did not like the cause more than at Carlisle'. Only one gentleman joined here, and he was a Catholic from Northumberland. Their reception at Kendal was less chilly, but again, no support was forthcoming.[48] No resistance occurred either and Jacobite demands for the funds belonging to local tax collectors were not refused.[49]

Support for the Jacobites in the counties of Cumberland and Westmorland was extremely limited. In all, five men from Cumberland joined the Jacobite ranks and none of them was a man of any standing.[50] A less ardent Jacobite was George Smith of Bothley, who had allegedly declared that George II ruined the nation by keeping mistresses. He also allegedly met the Jacobites and arranged quarters for them.[51] There was also a little verbal support. One George Taylor of Stapleton remarked on

19 November, 'I am very glad that Charles has got the victory', which was a reference to Prestonpans, eight weeks before. Another five men from the county were said to have either drunk success to the Jacobite cause or made other 'seditious' expressions.[52]

Although no effectual attempt was made in these counties to halt the main Jacobite army – and it is difficult to see how it could have been otherwise – loyalism was not extinct here. On 31 October, 120 loyal inhabitants of Penrith taken from all ranks of society had banded together 'with a resolution to do everything in our power to oppose the attempts of His Majesty's Enemies'. They were armed and had been training, but, alone and unaided could do little more and so stood down when the Jacobites arrived.[53] Loyalism also manifested itself in the collecting and disseminating of information. The Preston postmaster sent on news from Kendal on 22 November and he continued to do so on 26 November, when the Jacobites had arrived in Lancashire.[54] Yet when Lonsdale made reports, he could not vouch for them 'the common reports that fly about all these counties are so uncertain and generally speaking false'. On the following day he told Newcastle that the Jacobites numbered 7,000 men.[55]

There was some resistance to the Jacobites where it was possible. On 29 November, a small party of 20 Jacobites from Carlisle went to Lowther Hall, home of the absentee Lonsdale, via Penrith. On learning this news, Mr. Armitage, Lonsdale's steward, led a group of about 30 country people (perhaps taken from the 120 volunteers mentioned above), with makeshift weapons, to attack them there. After a fire fight, for the loss of one man wounded, they killed one Jacobite, injured three and took 11 prisoners, the remainder fleeing.[56] Armitage was uncertain as to the results of this action, fearing the Jacobites might seek revenge, but hoped their success would encourage others and that they would attack the Jacobites again, if possible.[57] On a smaller scale, when two Jacobites were found requisitioning horses, the animals were retaken by countrymen.[58]

Less successfully for the loyalists, there was a move in Carlisle to overthrow the garrison left there. This was the result of the alleged 'tyranny of an Highland government'. Groupings of men in the city and surrounding countryside began to plot against the occupying force, which was little over 100 men. A scheme was formed to seize the castle and defeat the Jacobites. Yet John Hamilton learnt of the plot, invited the mayor and aldermen to dinner and then secured them, only releasing the civic dignitaries when they promised to discourage all similar plans.[59]

Lancashire

Both sides had high hopes that Lancastrians would play a key part in the struggle; both were to be largely disappointed. There were two loyalist forces, the Liverpool Blues and the Lancashire Militia. Now was the time for action, and they behaved in contrasting fashions. Colonels William Graham and Alexander Gordon 'two pretty Gentlemen & very good soldiers' arrived in Liverpool on 10 November to take command of the Liverpool Blues there. A junior officer, Walter Shairp (1724–1787), noted that this was 'to our Great happiness & Joy at being no longer under the Direction of a parcel of Ignorant Aldermen'.[60]

Once the officers had arrived, their work could begin. Graham had the men parade on Town Field on 11 November and, at last, had them issued with muskets for, presumably, the first time. He decided to create an additional company out of the existing six so that his nephew might have a command. Each of the seven companies now had about 70 men. On the following day, the rest of the men's uniforms were delivered; blue coats, hats, shoes and stockings. On 13 November they underwent training in drill and musketry.[61]

The question was what to do next. Although Pritchard had thought in September that Liverpool needed 10,000 men to defend it, the corporation now decided that the regiment should defend the town against the Jacobite army, despite their numbers. This did not go down well with the regiment's officers. Shairp mocked the 'wise' corporation and their 'so Ridiculous a Scheme'. Graham was annoyed as he did not like being given a command and then being told he had to share that authority. The officers threatened to lay down their commissions if the corporation insisted on such a step as they stated their allegiance was to Graham and not to the corporation. The latter rethought the issue and allowed the regiment to march out of the town.[62] They marched from Liverpool on 15 November and arrived at Warrington on the following day. They then remained there for four days, awaiting orders.[63]

The Blues' opposition to the invaders was restricted to attempts to slow their march southwards by breaking bridges across which they would have to march. Cholmondeley sent an order on 24 November to the Liverpool Blues to break the bridge at Warrington over the Mersey in order to inhibit any Jacobite advance towards Chester.[64] This was done; the middle arches having been removed by the end of 24 November.[65] On 25 November, the Duke of Richmond, a regular army officer, was pleased to write 'I am glad to find they have broke down the bridge at Warrington and hope they will do the same at Stockport'.[66] They also destroyed Crossford bridge and Barton Bridge, too, though not that at Stockport as the Jacobite army was too close.[67] Then, with the arrival of the Jacobites in the county, they joined the garrison of regulars at Chester.[68] Some, such as the gentlemen of Stockport, did not approve of such bridge breaking because it would inconvenience local inhabitants and not disrupt the Jacobite advance, but their wishes were disregarded.[69]

It is worth noting the attitudes of the men in the unit towards an actual confrontation with the invaders. Shairp wrote that the regiment 'could be of no service in opposing the whole army when there was no forces near us to support us'.[70] Yet the force was not unenthusiastic when the prospect of danger loomed, as Shairp also noted on the occasion of what turned out to be a false alarm:

> However, this was of some service to us as it gave us an opportunity of trying the men's courage which was very extraordinary as not a man of them shewed the least sign of fear but went all on with the greatest alacrity altho' I believe evry one of them expected to be attacked that moment.[71]

Thus it would seem that the Liverpool men were brave but not suicidal. This should guard us against generalisations often made about apathy and unwillingness to fight the invaders which some historians have made.

Meanwhile, in Liverpool, men were raised to deter the Jacobites and others sent out to observe their march. On the scouts' return, they found the avenues to the city guarded, with the first floor of houses lit up and the second manned by armed men, ready to fire on any Jacobites. Yet with news that the Jacobites were marching towards Manchester, there was a great sense of relief.[72] It was fortunate that appearances masked reality, for, as Derby wrote, 'Liverpool is certainly not tenable'.[73]

The other force was the county militia. Despite differences of opinion among their leaders, the militia were eventually raised; to the number of seven companies – perhaps only about 500 men. Arms were gathered for their use and 14 days' pay was issued on about 12 November. Hoghton supported such a move, knowing that, though they could not stop the Jacobites, they could prevent any internal disturbance. The companies were initially stationed in Blackburn, Burnley, Colne, Clitheroe, Whalley and Preston. Derby was against such a policy because he reasoned that without regular troops the militia were of no use. Government and military suggestions about sniping at the Jacobites or obstructing their passage or denying supplies were looked upon with scorn. Morale was low. Derby's son wrote on 19 November that it had been 'an ill concerted scheme from the beginning'.[74]

The Lancashire Militia was unable to do anything effectual. Facing the Jacobites, who Derby knew were approaching the county, he wrote to Newcastle on 22 November 'In these circumstances, we are of opinion the best thing we can do is to secure as well as we can our arms from falling into the hands of our enemies'. Derby was unwell, with 'a body jaded almost to Death and an aching heart'.[75] Arms were stored aboard a ship at Liverpool. Derby concluded that 'a raw undisciplined militia consisting of Foot without anyone that knows how to command, should be able to prevent the advance of an army 7 or 8 times their number' was sheer folly. Had elements of the regular army reached the county before the Jacobites, the militia might have been of some use, but the regulars were no nearer than the Midlands.[76]

[Figure 20]
Dr. Henry Bracken
informs the Duke
of Newcastle about
the advancing
Jacobite army in
November 1745.
Reproduced by
permission of The
National Archives.
TNA, SP36/80,
f120r.

In any case, that 14 days' pay which had been advanced to the militia on 12 November would expire soon and with the general confusion in the county with the expected arrival of the Jacobites, no new funds would be forthcoming, so the men would disperse on 26 November. Both leaders and men went home on 24 November, the deputy lieutenants being unanimous in such a decision.[77] Hoghton retreated to his estates in Yorkshire but, as shall be seen, returned when he could be of some use. He had wanted the militia to accompany him, so that, kept together, they might be of some use, but this was not to be.[78] Derby told Richmond that he was going to London because 'not seeing how it is any way in my power or any of the friends of the government to be longer serviceable to the country in which my fortune lys, or the nation in general.'[79] This

action did not go down favourably with loyalists, for Derby was burnt in effigy 'for deserting them on this occasion'.[80]   However, Cholmondeley thought his behaviour was reasonable, 'it would be impossible for such a Body to make any Defence'.[81]

Loyalists sent news of the Jacobites to the government. Dr. Henry Bracken (1697–1764), a physician of Lancaster, sent information to Wade, with estimates of Jacobite strength. Bracken also had a nine or ten Jacobite stragglers arrested and sent a cache of letters found on one to London by express. On the Jacobites' arrival in Lancaster, the stout hearted doctor drank the King's health in their company – the invaders not realising he meant George II.[82] The Lieutenants also forwarded news that they thought might be useful to the government, whilst Cholmondeley passed on intelligence to Newcastle from customs officials in Wales, Lancashire and Cheshire.[83]

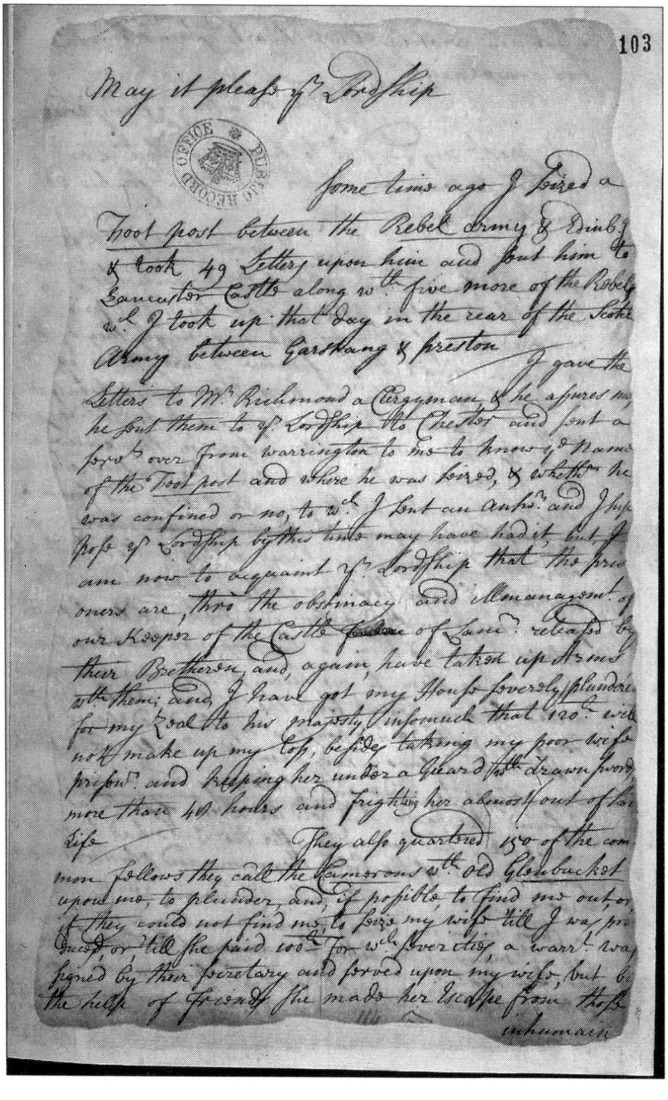

The magistrates and their agents were understandably reluctant to act against the Jacobites in this period, though some did. The Manchester constables took two or three stragglers from the Jacobite army and had them committed to the house of correction.[84] A Lancaster constable committed another prisoner, but the Preston JPs refused to take two from James Ray, a Whitehaven gypsy and future historian of the Forty Five, for fear of the Jacobites.[85] Elsewhere there was confusion leading to inaction. There was the proposal that gunpowder in Manchester should be removed and that initially the constables should foot the bill. They were understandably unhappy to do so and the proposal was made that the money used to finance the association be used instead.[86]

The responses of many officials was to do what the invaders wanted, albeit under duress. The Jacobites, following the precedent set in 1715, financed their war effort by collecting the taxes payable to George II's government; chiefly the Excise and Land Tax, from the towns they marched through.[87] At Preston such 'Public Money' was collected, at Manchester, the town's bellman had to give notice to all innkeepers and others with such money that they must appear before the Jacobites with their cash and accounts 'upon pain of military execution'.[88] In Lancaster, all talk of defending the castle was given up once Elcho told the mayor that the town would be safe if it was undefended.[89]

Although the Jacobites' march on Manchester led to the departure of the magistrates from the town, lesser civic dignitaries remained.[90] These included the town's constables; Thomas Walley and William Fowden. On the Jacobite arrival in Manchester, they were forced to attend them and to assist them in a number of tasks. These included the provision of labour to repair Crossford bridge, assisting with billeting troops and providing arms and ammunition, horses, carriages and hay. Fowden also had to proclaim Charles as Prince Regent.[91]

Both were most reluctant to undertake these tasks. When Fowden was summoned to appear before the Jacobites, he initially refused, but when a number came to him, armed, he had little choice. He was told to obey their instructions 'on pain of military execution'. Just before this, a Jacobite soldier drew his sword to leave Fowden in no doubt what this meant. Next day, this was reinforced, Fowden was told 'Sir, I charge you in Prince Charles's name to obey all our commands; if you refuse any of them you are a dead man and we'll lay your house in ashes and take your family prisoners'. Death was again referred to.[92] As Fowden had sworn allegiance to George II on taking his post of constable, he was reluctant to proclaim Charles. Yet 'he did [it] very unwillingly and in great fear'. He did his best to resist when he could, such as refusing to advise a plumber to make bullets.[93]

Some thought that the constables' behaviour was treasonable. It would seem, however, that Fowden and his colleagues were not only forced to act in the way in which they did but that they had the prior permission from the magistrates to act in such a fashion. Walley had asked Edward Chetham, a JP, what he and his fellow constables should do. Chetham replied 'that if the rebels forced them to do anything, they were to submit, but that he advised them to do nothing for them but what they were forced to, which direction they determined to follow'.[94]

With the civilian forces removed from the scene and the regulars still in the Midlands, the populace was wholly undefended. Many fled the Jacobite advance. The mayor of Lancaster departed when he learnt the news of the Jacobite approach.[95] Likewise the clergy: not one above the rank of curate stayed in the towns, lest they be forced to conduct divine service.[96] At Preston it was noted 'We are under the utmost apprehension here…it is not easy to express how much all ranks and degrees of people are frightened'.[97] So, too, the rector and parson of Wigan, who left town before their foes arrived. However, before laying low, the Rev. Lewthwaite preached in a militant tone 'He that has no sword, let him sell his garment and buy one'.[98] More passive resistance occurred when the Jacobites advanced southwards; the gentlemen at Preston being determined not to hand over any of the subscription money to them, and, as far is known, none was.[99] The Manchester postman took evasive action, too, 'we suppose to secure the money from falling into the hands of the rebels'.[100]

Should the absconding magistrates be accused of cowardice? Clearly, they shared the general fear of the rebels and concern for themselves, their families and their goods. But there was another motive. Senior figures, who, had they stayed, would have been forced to proclaim Charles as Prince of Wales and submit to him as a legitimate Prince. The corporation of Carlisle had had to do so, so why not those of Lancaster and elsewhere? However, their absence was to lead to a lack of any figureheads who could otherwise have rallied the populace against the Jacobites, once the Jacobites were not in the immediate vicinity.

Other loyalists fled, too. Mr. Whitworth, proprietor of the anti-Jacobite *Manchester Magazine*, left the town; and there was no edition of his newspaper published between 26 November and 17 December 1745.[101] He was not alone. Kay recorded on 28 November, 'How Persons are removing their Families and Effects out of Manchester. We have here [at Bury] a Numerous family'.[102] Those who could not or would not, flee, also took precautions. Again, Kay writes, but this time of his own family 'All Things are in a Hurry, Business is confus'd. We have conceal'd our valuables mostly, the Press has been so strong for Horses that for fear lest ours shou'd be seized we have sent them away to Day'. Friends from Manchester also stayed with the Kays at this uncertain time.[103] In Liverpool, valuables were packed aboard ships and then these ships were sent outside the docks. Families were sent over the Mersey into the Wirral.[104] Some fled as far afield as Chapel en le Firth in Derbyshire; those who could not flee hid their valuables.[105]

But not all fled. According to one account, though not by others, there was an attempt by some of Manchester's inhabitants to oppose the Jacobites on their arrival. This occurred when the first few of their number (one Dickson, his mistress and a drummer) arrived on 28 November. Although the three were unmolested at first, when the people realised they were alone, their actions changed, 'they surrounded him in a tumultuous manner, with the intention of taking him prisoner, alive or dead'.[106] However, Dickson kept them at bay with his blunderbuss until those favourable to the Jacobite cause in Manchester rescued him.[107] Others in Manchester failed to illuminate their windows on the following day in order not to show Jacobite loyalty; their windows were broken in consequence.[108]

Reactions in Lancashire varied from indifference to enthusiasm. According to Elcho, when the Jacobite manifesto was read at Lancaster, 'the people testify'd no joy and seemed all against the Cause'.[109] Yet elsewhere, there was encouragement. On the road to Preston, the Jacobites were met by 'two violers with their Fiddles playing the King Shall Enjoy his Own Again'.[110] At Preston the like continued. Elcho later wrote 'The people of Preston shew'd more Joy upon seeing the Prince Than they had done any where else, and their were for the first time in England several huzzas, and the next day when the manifestos were read the people asked for them and seemed keen to read them'. [111] O'Sullivan noted that men and women were eager to touch Charles, crying 'God blesse the king and the Prince'.[112] Likewise, Murray of Broughton recorded 'the Chevalier was mett by a great concourse of people and welcomed with the Loudest Shouts and acclamations of Joy'.[113]

Two Lancashire gentlemen joined the Jacobite cause. One was Francis Townley (1709–1746).[114] A Catholic, he apparently imbibed his family's Jacobitism at an early age and had then acquired military experience as an officer in the French army between 1728 and 1743. Apparently, he so 'distinguished himself in the cause' and so was given charge of the Manchester Regiment where he was 'exceedingly active in raising and disciplining the Regiment'.[115] The other was John Daniel, whose father had been an active Jacobite in 1715, and who explained why he was one, too:

> The lessons of loyalty, which had been instilled into me from my infant years, had made a deep and indelible impression upon my mind; and as I advanced towards maturity, and my reasoning facilities were developed, I became so firmly convinced of the solidity of the principles which I had been taught, that, when arrived at the age of Twenty two, I resolved never to deviate from them but to act. [116]

The only other support from the gentry was verbal. On the road, one squire Tidesley (a member of a Jacobite family) urged onlookers to 'help the Prince to his throne', whilst remaining a bystander himself. [117] Another gentleman was Edmund Starkie of Preston, who entertained Charles when he was in Preston.[118]

Responses to Charles himself were favourable. Daniel wrote 'the brave prince marching on foot at their head like a Cyrus or a Trojan Hero, drawing admiration and love from all hearts who beheld him, raising their long-dejected hearts, and solacing their minds with the happy prospect of another Golden Age'.[119] According to Beppy Byrom, 'a noble sight it is, I would not have missed it for a great deal of money…he was received with as much joy and shouting almost as if he had been king without any dispute, indeed I think scarce anybody that saw him could dispute it.'[120] Even the Rev. Richard Lluwellyn (1710–1770), who was not a Jacobite, wrote 'The young Pretender has marched all the way from Edinburgh on foot, and declares he will not stride a horse 'till he gets to St. James".[121] Yet opinions on his followers were rarely favourable. Dr. Bracken had a low opinion of the Jacobites, writing 'The common soldiers are a most despicable crew…low in stature and of a mean and meagre countenance'.[122]

Recruitment was limited, however, and was far less than it had been in 1715. For example, at supposedly Jacobite Preston, only eight joined.[123] Yet, on the road from Preston to Wigan, they were met by well wishers. None of these, however, offered to take up arms, even if offered them, on the grounds that 'they did not Understand fighting'.[124] Likewise, Murray of Broughton recorded that a few enlisted 'but no numbers as was expected'.[125] Daniel distributed Jacobite manifestos in Lancashire villages, but the reception was disappointing 'But alas! Not withstanding all our proposals and exhortations, few of them consented to join the Prince's army'. Yet Daniel persuaded 39 men to enlist.[126] By 27 November, there had been 60 recruits to the Jacobite cause.[127] Despite all the fears of Jacobitism in Lancashire, the Duke of Cumberland concluded, on 28 November 'there has not appeared any mark of disaffection even in that county'.[128] He was wrong, but he was not grossly so.

There was also a spontaneous mass outbreak of Jacobitism at Ormskirk – the only one to occur. Two hundred Catholics appeared there on the night of 25 November, with drums beating for Charles and then proclaiming him regent.[129] Yet the mob was dispersed resulting in about a dozen arrests.[130] Even so, Pelham, bearing in mind this outbreak, wrote 'I don't like [it] for tho' it was put an end to easily, it looks as if the Roman Catholics were further engaged than I thought'.[131] The Rev. Edward Daniel, brother to John Daniel reported that 30 to 40 Catholics of his congregation joined the Jacobites, but that was all.[132]

Yet Pelham's fears were exaggerated. John MacDonald, a Jacobite officer, asked a colleague, Sir Thomas Sheridan, about the state of Catholics in Lancashire, and whether the priests there had had correspondence with the Jacobite court. Apparently there had not been such discourse, because the

Jacobites were fearful of being associated with Catholics in the eyes of the British people who were mostly staunchly anti-Catholic.[133] Furthermore, the following remark, made in retrospect, is worth noting, 'the Romans in general behav'd themselves very dutifully throughout the county, even when the pretender was there'.[134]

If the county's Catholics were generally unenthusiastic, Lancashire Dissenters were mostly hostile. Daniel recorded that a Quaker harangued others in a public house that he was keeping the local Catholics quiet. However, Daniel later accosted him and threatened him into delivering up his weapons.[135] Richard Kay also records hostility. He made a number of comments about the need for spiritual correction and the hope for salvation, especially in November, praying that the 'Rebells, these rebellious Wretches' would be suppressed.[136] Practically, Kay's family did little, other than to conceal their valuables and to send their horses to a place of safety. Relatives came to stay with them.[137]

Manchester was a great goal for the Jacobites. It was believed to be a stronghold of Jacobitism. There had been Jacobite rioting there in 1715 and rumours of Jacobite sympathy there in late September 1745. That it was a potential centre of support was because it was not an incorporated town and so non-jurors – Anglicans who did not acknowledge the Hanoverians as the rightful monarchs – could legally inhabit the town. There were a number of non-jurors in Manchester and their support seemed probable.[138] Charles' officers assured him that 'they would be joined by all his English friends at Manchester'.[139] O'Sullivan thought that 'at least 1500 men' would have joined up.[140]

Once Colonel Pitsligo's Jacobite advance guard arrived on 28 November, they were met with a friendly mob, some of whom promised to enlist. With the arrival of the main army on the following day, there was more apparent support, especially when Charles himself arrived. According to Elcho:

> The Mob huzza'd him to his Lodgings, the town was mostly illuminated, and the Bells rung, their were several substantial People came and kis'd his hand, and a vast number of people of all sorts came to see him supp.[141]

However, as Elcho recorded, 'After all these proceedings it was natural enough to imagine that their would be a great joining, but everybody was astonish'd to find that all that was to join was about 200 Common fellows'. They were known as the Manchester Regiment, under Townley's command.[142]

The strength of the Manchester Regiment has been variously estimated; ranging from 150 to 300.[143] The definitive list numbers 188, though the complete figure must have been higher, due to desertions reducing the known number; perhaps a maximum strength of between 200 and 300 is

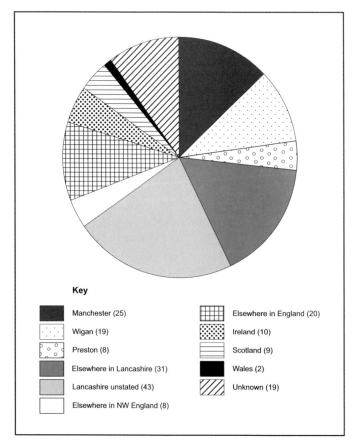

Key

▨ Manchester (25)	▦ Elsewhere in England (20)
⬚ Wigan (19)	▨ Ireland (10)
⬭ Preston (8)	▤ Scotland (9)
▨ Elsewhere in Lancashire (31)	■ Wales (2)
▨ Lancashire unstated (43)	▨ Unknown (19)
□ Elsewhere in NW England (8)	

[Figure 21]
Pie Chart showing
the known
whereabouts of the
men of the Jacobite
Manchester
Regiment. Chart
drawn by Simon
Chew.

realistic.[144] Of the 188 which are known about, only 25 definitely came from Manchester, with 101 from elsewhere in the county. There were 28 from other English counties, 21 from Scotland, Ireland and Wales, and 19 whose origins are unstated.[145] It seems likely that Jacobites from Lancashire and elsewhere came to Manchester to enlist. They were from mixed backgrounds. The largest contingent were the weavers, 32 in number; but there were also those from professional and even gentry backgrounds. We know more about these of some social standing, who became officers and were later tried for treason. Some were Catholics, such as Townley and Thomas Chadwick; but not all; the three sons of Dr. Thomas Deacon (1697–1753) of Manchester, a physician and non-juring bishop, enlisted. James Bradshaw was an Anglican, though from a Catholic family. James Dawson was Anglican, too. Among the officers, Anglicanism predominated, but among a partial list of the Englishmen in the ranks, Catholicism was dominant; 28 were Catholic, eight Anglican and of the other 56, there is no record.[146]

It is also worth noting that a number of Lancashire men joined up, but did not join the Manchester Regiment. Nineteen others from the county appear on prisoner lists, either as servants to Jacobite officers, having enrolled in other units, or as deserters from the regular army.[147]

The officers were generally well motivated Some had Jacobitism instilled at an early age, Thomas Sydall's father had been executed for his part in the Fifteen in 1716; the Deacons were non jurors, and Townley was not only a Catholic but had served in the French Army. As said, Daniel's father was a Jacobite and he gave his son his blessing.[148] On the scaffold, Jacobites made their political allegiances known. Thomas Chadwick said:

> I die an unworthy member of the Catholic Church which instructed
> me in the Principles of Loyalty to my sovereign, King James the third,

whom I pray God almighty bless...Great Britain will never prosper until the Royal Family be restored to their undoubted rights...German Counsels now prevail and this poor Island bleeds for the sake of a paltry insignificant territory.[149]

Some claimed that the common men who joined the Jacobite ranks did not do so out of any political or religious inclinations. Elcho claimed that they 'had no subsistance' and that 'they used to say by way of showing their military inclination, that they had for sometime been resolved to enlist with whichever of the two armies came first to town'.[150] A later writer noted that the rank and file was made up of 'Persons of abandoned Principles and desperate Fortunes'.[151] As already mentioned, they came from a variety of backgrounds, and in any case, regular armies themselves were usually made up of such men. The men themselves claimed that they were escaping bad masters, or had got drunk and found they had enlisted, or even that they only went along to safeguard property that the Jacobites had taken, or were forced to join them.[152] Yet to some extent, these may be excuses; Benjamin Bowker, deputy constable of Manchester, related 'The said several persons did not appear as people under any Restraint or Compulsion, but as free agents'.[153] There was at least one convinced Jacobite amongst them. One John Rowbotham, a Manchester carpenter and weaver, aged 35, who later confessed that his motivation had been due to 'Duty to God and my King and Country and in endeavouring to restore the House of Stuart who have been so long banished...whose right is indisputable to these three kingdoms'.[154]

It is also worth noting for all this alleged Jacobite rhetoric at the scaffold, many Jacobite prisoners tried to save their lives at their trials by pleading that they were not fervent Jacobites; that they had somehow become mixed up with them by accident. Much of the Jacobite rhetoric employed by each man was very similar and may not be genuine.[155]

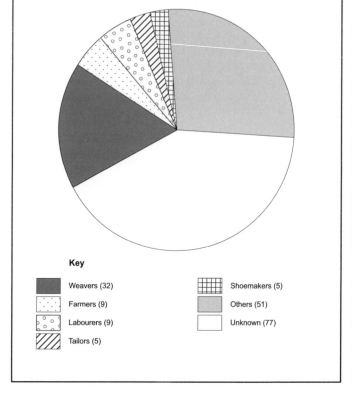

Key

Weavers (32)	Shoemakers (5)
Farmers (9)	Others (51)
Labourers (9)	Unknown (77)
Tailors (5)	

[Figure 22]
Pie Chart showing the known occupations of the men of the Jacobite Manchester Regiment. Chart drawn by Simon Chew.

All this encouraged Charles; but it cut no ice with some of his officers. The latter were unimpressed by what they termed '200 vagabonds' joining them and argued for a retreat, given the lack of support they had received in England. Yet they consented to carry on.[156] The number of men who joined was not high by any standards. The standard excuse was that there were 'unwilling to rise in arms against an established government, till they saw a body of regular troops actually land'.[157] Yet there had been at least 800 Englishmen who joined the Jacobites in 1715 and several thousand enlisted with Monmouth in 1685 to try and overthrow James II. All these causes failed, but it should also be recalled that no one knew that this was a cause which was to fail catastrophically. There was every reason to believe it would succeed and restore the Stuarts.

On a lesser note, several Lancastrians were later accused of seditious words. John Tomlinson, a Bury shoemaker, proposed Charles Stuart's health and Jeffrey Battersby of the same place said 'King George had no right to the Crown of England, but it belonged to the Stuart family and that no Hanoverian had any right to the Crown of England', adding 'Damnation to King George and success to Jimmy'. Michael Whitlock, a Manchester barber, said that George II had no right to the throne and would quickly lose it, drinking 'confusion to [the] Elector of Hanover and success to King James'.[158] John Hatton of Melling drank Jacobite healths, referring to King James and Prince Charles.[159] Joshua Winterbotham of Greenacre Moor sang 'O my Bonny, Bonny, Highland Ladie' outside Theophilius Ogden's house in Manchester.[160] More circumspect was John Cheshyre, who owned goblets adorned with Stuart emblems.[161]

Some men helped the Jacobites; one John Appleton went with them to Ashton to search for supplies.[162] Another such was the aforesaid Jeffrey Battersby, who helped collect the public money and freely gave the Jacobites his local knowledge of Bury.[163] Other local men were hostile. Samuel Cheetham, steward at Middleton Hall, claimed he would shoot any Jacobites, and, indeed, assaulted a Scottish pedlar. When a Jacobite party arrived, he had already hidden the family valuables, and insulted the Jacobites, shouting 'Gullook' at them.[164] Likewise, when Appleton and his party arrived at Ashton, one Henry Andrews yelled out 'Damne thee' and 'God Bless King George'.[165]

A number of clergy in Manchester showed their support towards the Jacobites, in varying degrees. The most prominent was Thomas Coppock, who had been born in 1719 and had later attended Brasenose College, Oxford, had joined the Jacobite army at Manchester and, logically enough, became the chaplain to the Manchester Regiment. In his clerical capacity he had officiated at Derby parish church and prayed for James as King and his sons as Prince Regent and Duke of York in a number of churches. At Manchester he preached a sermon with the text from Psalms XCVII, 1, 'The Lord is King, may be glad thereof'.[166] Yet his duties were also secular.

Coppock had encouraged others to join the Jacobite army and had acted as quartermaster, arranging billets in Manchester. Along the route he was treated as an officer, wore a white cockade and was armed.[167]

Coppock's Jacobitism seems certainly to have been genuine. At his execution, he stated that his epitaph would be 'The only English Protestant Clergyman, whose Honour, zeal, courage and loyalty, were conspicuous in his royal master's cause'. He talked of the tyranny and corruption of the present government and the usurping family, as compared to the princely virtues of the Stuarts. Coppock argued that he had followed the doctrine of the Anglican Church as it was prior to the Revolution, avoiding both extremes of Catholicism and fanaticism. Yet we should note that at his trial, he disowned his Jacobite principles.[168]

Coppock was certainly not alone in his Jacobite sympathies. A number of Lancashire clergymen shared his sentiments. Elcho recalled that in Manchester, on Charles' arrival, 'Their were likewise some Clergymen of the Church of England came and waited upon him & one of them joined, and ever after in all the towns and villages where the army was and where their was a Church he used to say prayers And Pray publickly for the Prince and all his family.'[169] The clergyman in question was, of course, Coppock, but there were clearly others.

One of these was the Rev. John Clayton (1708–1773), once (as with Coppock) of Brasenose College, and now chaplain at the non-juring Collegiate Church of Manchester (both reputed hotbeds of Jacobitism), who went with the boys of Salford Grammar School to pay their respects to Charles when he passed through Salford and saluted a Jacobite officer. In the following year, his scholars joined in a Jacobite riot and shouted 'Down with the Rump' and threw stones at their opponents.[170] Clayton was later charged with having spoken against George II.[171] Equally public in his Jacobitism was the Rev. Thomas Cattell, also of Manchester. He had once been a member of a Jacobite club and had 'no loyalty to spare for Germany', meaning, of course, for George II. Both Clayton and Cattell eagerly went to wait upon Charles at Manchester on 30 November and Clayton said grace at his table. On the same day, the church bells (presumably of the Collegiate Church) rang for Charles; another very public indication of Jacobite loyalty.[172]

Even more circumspect in his Jacobitism was the non-juring John Byrom, who went to consult how to avoid 'any scrape, yet behave civilly' and then had to be 'fetched prisoner' before he met Charles. Dr. Deacon was also rather ambiguous. He met Charles at his Manchester lodgings, though, as with Byrom, he did so reluctantly. But he was also reported as having drunk the following health in front of a number of Jacobites 'Here's wishing your Prince's Good health and Success to you all.' Earlier he had spoken to one Dr. Hopwood about being obliged to join the Jacobites unless given a special dispensation not to do so due to his large family.[173]

And, as noted, his three sons joined the Jacobite forces and became junior officers in the Manchester Regiment, though this was given out as being against their father's consent. Although Deacon had done nothing in public that his enemies could accuse him of, this was not quite the same as being innocent.[174] Mr. John Shrigley of Manchester omitted the names of the royal family to be prayed for during a service at Manchester on 30 November, which, of course, could be the sign of a cautious Jacobite, or of a man who was just cautious.[175] As noted earlier, Waugh took a dim view of such ambiguity and inferred it was closet Jacobitism.

The equivocal nature of some of these Manchester Jacobites is well summed up in Byrom's rhyme:

[Figure 23]
Reluctant Jacobite:
John Byrom, M.A.,
by G. Clint, 1770.
Ref no. m72550.
Reproduced by
permission of
Manchester
Archives and Local
Studies Library.

'God Bless the King! I mean the Faith's Defender!
God bless (no harm in blessing) the Pretender!
But who Pretender is, and who is King –
God bless us all – that's quite another thing'.[176]

Such cautious behaviour did not aid the Jacobite cause one iota, understandable as it was for essentially peaceful men like Byrom. The role of the Jacobite clubs at Rochdale and Walton le Dale is also unknown. Had any of the Jacobites witnessed the scenes in Manchester subsequent to their departure, they might have realised how tenuous was their hold on power and how quickly their opponents would be able to reassert themselves. As soon as the Jacobite army had left Manchester on 1 December, resident Jacobites had their windows broken. [177]

Cheshire

On 1 December, the Jacobites marched southwards from Manchester through Cheshire and then Staffordshire. Some had thought their route would have been to the south west, via Chester and into Wales to attract support from there and Cholmondeley reported, on 20 November 'great commotions may be expected upon the further advance of the Rebels'. Instead they marched through Altrincham, Macclesfield and Congleton.[178]   Lacking hindsight, Cholmondeley had been busy in the county, trying to make the best possible preparations for defence.

These had been ongoing for several weeks. On 12 November, the Chester magistrates decided to block Castlegate and to do likewise to the city's other portal, or to repair them for the city's defence.[179] Buildings near to the walls were pulled down. A week later, householders were ordered to lay in a fortnight's food supplies.[180] Cholmondeley, as governor of the castle, 'began all proper dispositions for the defence of the city', causing one veteran and two newly raised regiments (including his own) to be moved into the castle and city. The walls and gateways were patrolled night and day.[181] The county magistrates were requested to make enquiries about wheat, hay, oats and straw for the garrison.[182]

[Figure 24]
Dr Charles Deacon, 1760. Image no. m72887. Reproduced by permission of Manchester Archives and Local Studies Library.

Yet Cholmondeley was pessimistic, only having two gunners and most of his troops were newly raised. He declared on 17 November that the town was indefensible for half a day even against a 'wild Rabble'. He thought that 'The only remedy left in such an Exigency…is the breaking down the Bridges'. However, the government were of the opinion that such 'might be attended with great inconveniencies'. Newcastle thought that such might however impede the Jacobite advance.[183] Yet Cholmondeley told him 'I am in such as perpetual hurry preparing for the defence of this place'.[184] The state of the defences certainly gave cause for concern – Brigadier Douglas remarked that the walls were overlooked by houses in the outer suburbs, that the castle was 'a very weak place', that its guns lacked gunners and the garrison was not to be depended upon.[185] Cholmondeley employed 800 men to deepen the ditches, throw up earthworks and erect sandbags

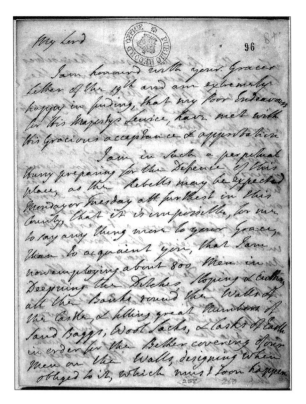

[Figure 25]
The Earl of
Cholmondeley
describes defensive
preparations made
at Chester in
November 1745.
Reproduced by
permission of The
National Archives.
TNA, SP36/73,
f255r.

and casks to make a parapet for the defenders, but he was convinced that such would only hold up the enemy by a week.[186]

Cholmondeley was initially eager to break down bridges to delay the march of the Jacobite army.[187] Yet, because the rivers in Lancashire were easy to ford, he thought that breaking bridges would be pointless, and 'it is impossible for us in this part of the world to think of doing anything towards stopping or impeding their march'.[188] However, as previously noted, three bridges were broken by the Liverpool Blues.

The people of Cheshire, as in Lancashire, felt threatened. At Chester, 'almost all the principal inhabitants, having sent away their goods, and most valuable moveables, retired to several parts of the county, the shops were shut up, and all trades, and business ceased for some weeks and things appeared with a melancholy aspect'.[189] On 2 December, Cholmondeley wrote 'such is the panick of the common people, which they catch from others of higher Rank…those, who have called themselves the King's Friends, have been the first to fly, and have, by that means, spread Terrors, and Apprehensions in all Parts'.[190] One of these was Peploe. He had written, on 10 November, 'that God would be pleased to put a happy end to this wicked Rebellion'. He left Chester.[191] He told Newcastle in the following July 'For the last seven months I have removed very little from my habitation'.[192] Peploe and his family had fled on hearing of the Jacobite march southwards 'which was expensive to me', paying for 14 or 15 soldiers, which may have acted as a bodyguard.[193] Another to escape was the Earl of Warrington who fled from Dunham Massey as the Jacobites advanced.[194] If removal were impossible, goods were concealed – the parish of St. Mary's, Chester, spent three shillings on 'securing church books and plate at ye time of the Rebellion'.[195]

Although there were complaints about the magistrates, the people of Cheshire appear loyal enough; some people being more zealous than the magistrates. One Mr. Furnivall of Congleton wrote 'Magistrates do not well receive the complaints of their Neighbours nor readily acknowledge their own Remissness'. JPs sent notes to have the roads repaired for the regular troops, but little regard was made to such requests.[196] John Nock of Knutsford claimed 'ye Protestants of Lancashire and Cheshire being strong and zealous in His Majesty's Interest', but could do nothing without weapons. Had they being armed, 'I doubt but 20,000 would be ready to take up the same in Defence of his Royal person'.[197] Elsewhere, civilians were receptive to soldiers in their midst. On 19 November, on the arrival of regulars to Chester, when the men were met halfway by a torch lit possession and an 'Extraordinary Reception and free entertainment thro' every town they pass'd, especially at my Town of Namptwich'.[198] It was also noted that the townsmen of Chester took in soldiers voluntarily and provided for them.[199]

The constables in at least some parishes were busy. Some acted against Catholics and helped with army transport. At Capesthorne, they undertook six searches in 1745–6 and provided some carriages to carry army baggage.[200] Those of Over Peover claimed expenses for warrants concerning lists of Catholics and travelled to Knutsford to bring back wagons used to carry army baggage.[201] Those at Barthomley not only saw to the transport of military luggage from Nantwich to Northwich, but repaired and cleaned muskets.[202]

But if they could not physically resist the invaders, they were busy in sending news of them to others. Nock referred to his town sending a messenger to Warrington to spy on the Jacobites.[203] Furnivall did similarly.[204] The latter sent fresh news on 2 December, as the Jacobites advanced from Macclesfield. He was of high spirits 'Our apprehensions of them seems now to be over. They seem to be in a great confusion'.[205] Samuel Cooper, mayor of Macclesfield, gave intelligence of the Jacobite march to an advanced party of regulars.[206]

The Jacobite advance ignored Chester and marched through Macclesfield instead. Again, as at Carlisle, the mayor and two or three aldermen in their gowns were obliged to proclaim the Stuarts as rightful Kings and then this was repeated by the town clerk. Cooper was also ordered to provide the Jacobites with bakers and bread.[207] But, as at Carlisle, the populace was unenthusiastic. According to Elcho 'at Macclesfield, the people seemed mightily against the Prince and vast numbers of people had run away from their houses'.[208] Threats had to be used to try and obtain the land tax books from the collector's wife – the tax collector, William Baxter, having fled beforehand. Cooper claimed that handing over money was 'greatly against his inclination' but, as with the Carlisle magistrates and Manchester constables, he and his colleagues were threatened with 'military execution'.[209] When the loyalist agent, James Ray, entered the town shortly after the Jacobites left, Cooper was happy to welcome him and gave him hospitality on the condition that Ray leave his arms in the inn, lest Cooper's house be fired.[210] David Browne, once town clerk, later recalled, 'it was then too hazardrous to remove my family, so determined to stand my ground, especially as my wife seemed to be in good spirits and in no way afraid. And indeed, I must own that she had more courage than all the whole family besides'.[211]

As with the two most northerly counties, Cheshire gave little support to the Jacobite cause. At Stockport Bridge, a number of Cheshire gentry welcomed Charles to their county. Among them was one Mrs. Skyring, an elderly lady who had, as a tiny child, seen Charles II arrive at Dover in 1660. She had devoted her life to the Stuarts, praying for their return, and had sent them half her income. She gave Charles her jewellery and plate.[212] Other support came from John Whitaker, a yeoman, who helped the Jacobites search for arms in Macclesfield, and one John Wadeson who attested to the rights of the Stuarts.[213] Five men from Cheshire enlisted with the Jacobites, which was the same number as in Cumberland.[214] The Legh family owned Jacobite drinking glasses, but declined to take any more active part.

Marching through Leek and Ashbourne, the Jacobites managed to avoid Cumberland's army based at Lichfield by means of a feint on the part of Lord George's command, and reached Derby on 4 December, having side stepped the only regular army in their vicinity. They then faced their most difficult decision. Although they had met little resistance in their entire march, their experiences in the north west were to be of crucial importance in making that decision.

Conclusion

The Jacobites had faced little effective resistance in their march through the four north-western counties and some historians have seen this as evidence for apathy among the alleged loyalists. Yet it is difficult to know what else could have happened, as the militia at Carlisle, in Lancashire and the Liverpool Blues were all small forces, numbering in their hundreds, and the Jacobite army was about 5,000 strong. Resistance was thus impossible. Another reason for the limited amount of popular resistance was because the Jacobites did not loot, despite all the propaganda to the contrary. This was unnecessary. As has been said, local tax collectors were relieved of their funds; as at Kendal, Preston and Manchester. Yet when it was possible to damage the Jacobite cause, by sending intelligence, attacking small parties and destroying bridges, efforts were made, mostly successfully. For the Jacobites, though, recruitment had been disappointing, and as the support promised by Charles failed to materialise, matters loomed ominously for the Stuart cause.

CHAPTER THREE

December 1745

On 4 December, the Jacobite army reached Derby. There was discussion on the following day whether to march to London or to retreat. More ink has been spilt on this topic than any other in Jacobite history. On the one hand, the regular armies had been out-marched (Cumberland was at Lichfield and Wade was in Yorkshire) and London was about 123 miles away. Charles, as ever, was adamant about the necessity to advance. Others disagreed, pointing to the lack of any substantial English support, which Charles had spoken of as being paramount and imminent throughout the last few weeks. There were a number of comments about this.

Ray wrote:

> The Disappointment they had met with in the Augmentation of their Forces; for they Flatter'd themselves with a great Insurrection in England in their Favour; Lancashire being the Place most depended upon, as appear'd by their Letters, for imaginary Succours; which County they had gone through without receiving the expected Supplies, few having join'd them, and those as I have already describ'd, People of desperate Fortunes and vile Principles.[1]

A similar account comes from Lluwellyn:

> I told you that 60 Persons had enlisted with the Pretender at Manchester, but was informed on the Spot that he had not half that number. I should not have thought it worth while to set you right in this Matter, but for its being a convincing Proof of the Nation's being well affected and attached to the present establishment.[2]

It was not necessarily active support which was required. As Lord George Murray remarked 'if their was any party in England, for him, it was very odd they had never so much as Either sent him money or intelligence or the least advice what to do'.[3]

Of course, there were other factors to be taken into consideration, such as the erroneous belief that there were a number of armies, totalling 30,000 men, about to close in on the Jacobites. Yet, had there been more support from Jacobites in the north west, the clan chieftains and regimental officers

WILLIAM AUGUSTUS,
late Duke of Cumberland.

[Figure 26]
Hero of the loyalists: William Augustus, late Duke of Cumberland, c.1765. Reproduced by permission of Carlisle Library.

might have overcome their concerns and have had restored their earlier faith in Charles' veracity. It was not to be, and the decision was taken to retreat. Whether this was the correct choice is debatable, at least in retrospect, as it is possible that a successful French invasion on the south coast, mass English support near to or in the capital, and military success over Cumberland's army, could have happened, culminating in a second Stuart restoration – or a bloody defeat.[4] As the Lancastrian Jacobite, John Daniel honestly observed 'How far they acted amiss or well in this, I know not'.[5]

On 6 December, the Jacobite army turned back. News of this momentous decision did not reach Cumberland until 7 December. He set off in pursuit on the following day, hoping to bring the Jacobites to battle in England but, aware that their army was faster moving than his own, he gathered together an advance guard composed of all his cavalry and mounted infantry. The Jacobites used the same route as they had in the previous month, only in reverse. Wade's army, now in Yorkshire, was directed to march westwards and cut off the Jacobite retreat in Lancashire.[6]

As with the previous chapter, this chapter is divided according to chronology and geography. As the armies marched through Cheshire and Lancashire first, these two counties will be dealt with in the first half, before proceeding to examine what occurred in Cumberland and Westmorland. Unlike the previous month, the people of the north west now had to respond to both the Jacobite army and the regular forces.

Cheshire and Lancashire

Cumberland's troops began to pursue the retreating Jacobites on 8 December. In order to try and catch up with their quarry, Cumberland wrote to the magistracy of the north west, urging them to slow down the Jacobite retreat. Yet little official action was possible because of the disarray the Jacobite march south had caused. As noted in the previous chapter, the Lancashire militia had been disbanded (Derby was in London and Hoghton in Yorkshire), so it could do nothing to hinder the retreating Jacobites. Similarly, the Cumberland and Westmorland militia had been disbanded after the surrender at Carlisle. The Cheshire militia was never embodied as Cholmondeley had concentrated on the defence of Chester. The Lancashire JPs had decamped before the Jacobite advance.[7] Lonsdale thought that not

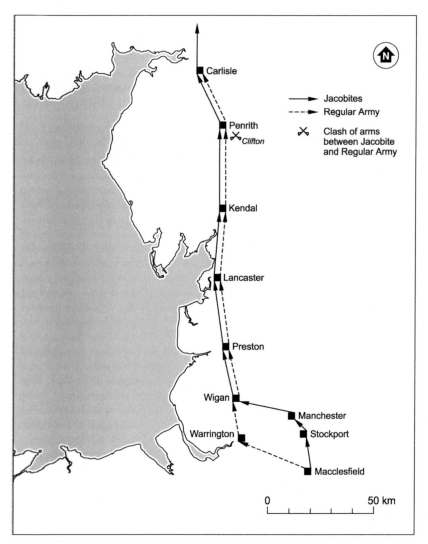

[Map 4]
Map showing the Jacobite retreat and the pursuit of the regular army through the North West of England in December 1745. Map drawn by Simon Chew.

much could be done, as there was little chance that the regulars would overtake the Jacobites. Even if they were able to do so, due to the mountainous terrain and few inhabitants, any work to retard the Jacobite retreat would be minimal.[8]

The failure of the militia to harass the retreating Jacobites received official censure from Sir Everard Fawkener, Cumberland's military secretary. Writing from Preston on 16 December, he thought that there were 'in this county a number of fine bodys of men of a very good spirit', yet he noted that no attempt had been made to hold the Jacobites in the passes in order that they might have allowed the regulars to come at them. He put this down to the lack of local leadership 'I imagine there is a want of spirit or understanding, or good intentions among the gentry'. He especially blamed Derby's 'irreconcilable Quitting of this county' as being responsible for such a state.[9] Yet, given the collapse of the militia only a few weeks previously, the flight of their leaders and the removal of their weapons on board ship, it is difficult to see what else could have happened.

Loyalists were obliged to flee when the Jacobites returned, especially if they had already acted against the Jacobites. At Lancaster, both Dr. Bracken and the Vicar, Dr. Fenton, fled before they arrived. Both had their houses ransacked.[10] Similarly Cooper of Macclesfield fled on learning the Jacobites were returning, though one man in that town shot a plundering Jacobite dead. A Macclesfield alderman fled with all his household but one elderly servant.[11]

Yet, in contrast to this, Colonel Yorke also thought the people were opposed to the Jacobites. He wrote from Preston on 15 December that:

If the good wishes of the poor country people and their prayers will avail anything, we have a good chance of succeeding, for never were the

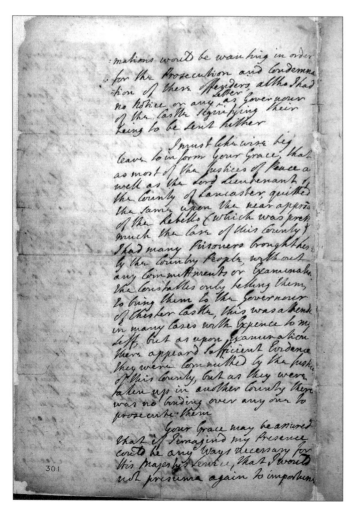

[Figure 27]
Dr. Henry Bracken notes that the Lancashire magistracy has fled the county in December 1745. Reproduced by permission of The National Archives. TNA, SP36/81, f298v.

people more hearty on any cause than they are in ours, and I don't doubt will be of infinite service to us in our expedition, for they recently have had some smart skirmishes with the rebels on their return.[12]

However, though there certainly was some irregular opposition to the Jacobites, it was of limited effect. There was a plan that the country people should rally at Manchester in order to oppose the Jacobites. Certainly the Kay family gathered about 500 people from Rossendale on 8 and 9 December for this purpose, and apparently thousands of others gathered there. Dr Edward Mainwaring (1710–1780) and Justice Bradshaw in the town itself rallied the populace and encouraged them to arm.[13] These arms were makeshift – scythes and hedge stakes, and allegedly, but impossibly, they numbered 11,000 men.[14] According to James Maxwell, the mob had turned aggressive because they had heard a rumour that the Jacobites had been defeated.[15]

The reception of the Jacobites in Manchester on 9 December was, therefore, rather different, to that of little over a week previously. According to Ray, 'they were not received as they had been before, nor have I heard that the new made officers had the Compliments paid them as usual on such Occasions, but on the Contrary, the Town's People, or at least, the Mob, gave them some pretty visible Marks of their Dislike'. Jacobite quartermasters, arriving in advance of the army, were forced to flee.[16] Yet when the Jacobite advance guard arrived, the loyalists fled. Maxwell recorded:

> There had been a good deal of mobbing and confusion in Manchester the day before. The Hanoverian mob, reinforced by great numbers of country people in arms had been very outrageous to the Prince's friends and seemed determined to dispute his passage, but upon the first appearance of the Prince's vanguard, the mob was dispersed.[17]

When the army arrived, such behaviour led to a fine of £2,500 being imposed on the town, which was promptly paid on the following day.[18] Other inhabitants fled or hid their valuables.[19] The loyalists became more aggressive when the Jacobites began to depart. Clods of earth were thrown at the retreating Highlanders in Manchester and they were fired upon, but once the rear guard threatened them, they ran away.[20]

Once the Jacobites had left Manchester for the second time, loyalists returned and acted in a variety of fashions. One of those who returned was Mainwaring, who soon afterwards preached 'a most furious sermon against Popery' and 'abuses them [the Highlanders] most strangely'. Others, on their return 'grew rather too valiant'. Windows of local Jacobites, such as Dr. Deacon, were broken (Deacon himself fled before the regulars arrived).[21] The constables sent an express to Cumberland to let him know of the Jacobite retreat and paid watchmen to stop anyone in the town sending news of his advance to the Jacobites.[22]

With the arrival of the regulars on 12 December, bonfires were lit, bells were rung and the town was lit up to welcome them.[23] Even some Manchester Jacobites were not unimpressed at their presence. Beppy Byrom recorded that the officers billeted upon them 'are very civil'. Loyalists, such as Mainwaring, were eager to meet Cumberland.[24] Some Jacobites decided to leave Manchester at this point; Dr. Deacon was one of these.[25]

But if the mass of loyalists at Manchester and elsewhere were ultimately cautious, a number of more deadly incidents were reported. At Stockport, country people fired from a village at night against a Jacobite patrol, and apparently 'killd some of them'.[26] Then there was a woman and her child. Before the Jacobites arrived in Manchester, these two came across a young English recruit to the Jacobite army. Between them, they cut his throat.[27] There was also a would-be assassin, as O'Sullivan recorded being fired upon near Wigan. [28]

Enthusiasm towards the regular army was evident. At Macclesfield, they were provided with quarters, provisions and straw 'with great chearfulness and readiness'.[29] Local farmers dug up the barrels of beer which they had hidden from the Jacobites and treated the regulars.[30] All this is more remarkable because of the English people's usual antipathy towards soldiers in their midst. Cumberland wrote 'I have the pleasure in finding the greatest of zeal...on the arrival of the King's troops'.[31] Warrington notables accompanied Cumberland on his march as far as Wigan.[32]

Churches throughout the region rang their bells to salute the regulars. St. John's Macclesfield rang '3 days when the Duke of Cumberland was here'.[33] At Stockport, an item in the accounts for £1 reads 'To the Ringers ringing two days and a half when the King's Troops went through the Town in pursuit of the Rebels in their retreat from Derby'.[34] Further north, the bells of Standish church rang 'when the Duke of Cumberland marched past with the Army'.[35]

There were other examples of loyalist action. Captain Dudley Bradstreet, a government agent, wrote that a rash loyalist made a toast to King George within Jacobite hearing.[36] Bradstreet, who needed to send messages to Newcastle, found some individuals in Lancashire willing to abet him. An elderly servant in Macclesfield who declared 'I will do anything in my Power to serve the King', passed on a message from Bradstreet to a neighbouring magistrate.[37] On the following day the curate of Standish was likewise approached and sent letters to Newcastle on Bradstreet's behalf, free of charge.[38]

Some corporations, notably Liverpool, assisted in the provisioning of the army on its pursuit. The mayor of Liverpool asked Cumberland if horses and provisions could be supplied 'for the more speedy march of the

Army'.[39] Eleven carts loaded with biscuits were despatched on 12 December.[40] The army thanked him as this act demonstrated 'a very considerable zeal upon this occasion'.[41] At Lancaster, the army was supplied with 77 bags of bread.[42]

Some in Lancashire reacted more militantly. It was claimed that Lancaster men had armed themselves with scythes, forks, guns and swords in order to do so, perhaps being encouraged by comments in the press referring to the Jacobites as 'A parcel of shabby, lousy, shitten, scoundrels'.[43] One Mr. Eccles and his neighbours 'determining not to be plundered any more by stragglers, armed themselves and stood upon their guard'. When a Mr. Dickenson, a Jacobite, approached their property one night, he was taken by the 'very angry' Mr. Eccles and friends.[44] Likewise, at Leighton, following reports of plundering by retreating Jacobites, 'ye country people thereabouts had armed themselves as best they could and had obliged ye dogs to sheer off'. When Cumberland's advance guard were four miles away, it was additionally stated 'the whole country are in arms and barricading ye roads especially between Lancaster and Kendal'.[45] Another manifestation of popular hostility occurred in Prescot, where townsmen and farmers to the number of 100 armed themselves with scythes, pitchforks, guns and rusty swords. They picked up over 40 stragglers, though this was no heroic feat, as many of the Jacobites were 'lame and almost dead'.[46]

Some Lancastrians became bystanders. Kay and others were curious to see the Jacobites and anyone in highland dress, so went to see them march from Manchester to Wigan on 10 December. On the following day they went to Manchester to see the men of Cumberland's army in pursuit. Kay commented on the latter with great approval 'It gives Abundance of Joy to good people to all true Protestants to see such a number of Fine Forces'.[47]

In the wake of the Jacobite retreat in late December, some people had taken the opportunity to round up Jacobite sympathisers and gain official kudos in doing so. Hoghton sent Newcastle the examination of a Charles Douglas and put one Morgan, who had worn a white cockade at Manchester, in gaol. He was thanked thus 'the King…is extremely sensible of this instance, and of the many other proofs, you have given on occasion for the present rebellion, of your constant care and attention to His Majesty's service'.[48] A newspaper reported that 30 to 40 men had been taken in Lancashire.[49]

One might have expected that local Jacobite sympathisers would have laid low after the Jacobite army retreated, but not a bit of it. When the Kays were raising the Rossendale men, an anonymous letter was sent to them, referring to their followers as 'a new Regiment of Rossendale Plunderers under the Emphatical Denomination of Oliverian Murderers'.[50] Bradstreet recorded that the Jacobite officers were 'all magnificently entertained by a beautiful Lady…She had the greatest desire to kiss the Rebel Prince's

Hand'.[51] A few men even enlisted with the Jacobites on their retreat from Derby.[52] Yet some of the Lancashire recruits probably took this opportunity to desert – as previously noted, the Manchester Regiment numbered about 200–300 men and only 188 are listed as prisoners. It was alleged that the adjutant of this unit, Thomas Sydall, wrote to his wife, informing her that 'there was nothing but death and confusion before them'. Yet he stayed with his men to the last.[53]

Generally speaking, the pursuit had not gone well for Cumberland. He had had to stay in Macclesfield for two days because of the possibility he would have to call off the pursuit entirely in order to confront a French invasion in the south of England. The Jacobite army had had little serious trouble from the country people of the north west and so had not been delayed. They reached Preston on 11 December, whereas Cumberland was at Manchester on 11 December. The Jacobite army had also outmarched Wade's army, which was at Wakefield on 10 December, too far away to cut them off.[54] This state of affairs was to change as they marched further north.

Westmorland and Cumberland

Resistance to the Jacobites on their march northwards through Westmorland and Cumberland in December was more visible than it had been in November. Why was there such militant resistance against the Jacobites at this stage of their retreat northwards? Was it just that they appeared to be losing and their attackers decided to be opportunistic and in attacking them join the winning side? Perhaps this was true to an extent. But there were other factors at play.

Firstly, there was the fact that the Jacobites were less law abiding when it came to personal property than they had been on the march south, as only the tax collectors' funds had been confiscated on that occasion. Thus popular animosity was inflamed which had not been the case previously. Daniel records that the Jacobite army's exemplary behaviour on their march southwards was not repeated on their march northwards:

> The Army irritated by the frequent instances of the enemy's malice began to behave with less forbearance. And now few they were, who would go on foot when they could ride; and mighty taking, stealing, and pressing of horses there was amongst us, for none of us was ever sure of keeping his own.[55]

News of such hostility spread and was increasingly exaggerated in the telling. Arthur Jessop, a Holmfirth apothecary, noted on 6 December 'They say that the Rebels are vastly more cruel and inhuman since they left Preston and Manchester'.[56]

But more importantly, it was now possible to attack the Jacobites with a possibility of success. With rumours of the Jacobites being defeated and that they were merely an army in pieces, small local forces had a reasonable chance. Buoyed up with false hopes, the men of southern Lancashire and those in and around Penrith and Kendal, attempted to take action against the Jacobites. Rumours of Jacobite defeats had spread and were recounted by Jessop on several occasions in December.[57] Likewise, Beppy Byrom wrote 'we have abundance of lies about them, they are killed, taken, surrounded, and got clean away, all two or three times of a day'.[58]

The proximity of the regular army also gave encouragement, as Colonel Yorke wrote, 'The country all up ready to join us and assist us against the rebels, now they saw themselves supported by the King's troops'.[59] Lonsdale was less hopeful, though, writing on 17 December that as the regulars had been two days behind the Jacobites, 'I can have very little expectation from their feeble attempts'.[60]

Thirdly, the population were encouraged to attack the Jacobites by the Duke of Cumberland. He asked that the 'people be incouraged to attack and harass them [the Jacobites] in passes or places of advantage'. He also suggested that the country people to deal with the Jacobite stragglers thus 'I did not care to put them [the Jacobites] to death, but I have encouraged the Country People to do it, as they shall fall into their hands'.[61]

That there was an aggressive spirit shown towards the Jacobites is evident. Jacobite memorialists certainly claim the people were desirous of harming them on their retreat, though not always effectively. Daniel wrote:

The Enemy…to endeavour to raise the inhabitants of the towns through which we had to pass against us, by spreading false reports, that the Prince's Army had been defeated…This report was believed…and every man thought himself capable of knocking out a Rebel's brains with a club or a staff. Then you might see heroic behaviour displayed among cocks that never crowed but among hens upon their own dunghill.[62]

Similarly, Johnstone remarked 'They were deficient neither in hatred towards us, nor in the wish to injure us, but they wanted courage and resolution to expose themselves to the swords of the highlanders'. Likewise, he noted 'Our stragglers seldom failed to be attacked by the English peasants, who were all implacable enemies of the Prince'.[63]

Once sufficient Jacobite numbers were gathered, little could be done. It was reported, on 16 December, that, though the 'whole country was all in arms, but on the approach of the rebels, were obliged to make the best of their way home, as they had but few soldiers to head them'.[64]

Perth's advance guard of cavalry, about 100 strong, was attacked in Kendal at ten in the morning on 14 December. Seeing that the troops

PRINCE CHARLIE'S HOUSE

Built in 1690, this house was owned during the Stuart rebellion of 1745 by Justice Thomas Shepherd. It was slept in by 'Bonnie Prince Charlie' during his advance on London and again during his retreat when his pursuer, the Duke of Cumberland, slept in the same bed on the following night. In an exchange of fire with the retreating army a highlander and a local farmer were shot.

KENDAL CIVIC SOCIETY

[Figure 28] Plaque commemorating the skirmish at Kendal in December 1745. Photograph by the author (2004).

arrived 'in great haste', it was believed they were in flight following a defeat. Furthermore, it was market day and a great number of people were assembled in the town. As the cavalry were reaching the bridge in the centre of town, their rearguard was mobbed by the crowd. A shot was fired from a window and one of Perth's hussars was killed. Returning fire, the hussars killed a shoemaker and an ostler. Although the crowd was dispersed, two hussars were taken prisoner.[65] The final death toll was four; Richard Toulman and Archibald Armstrong, both of Highgate, 'killed by ye Rebels' buried on 15 November and John Slack of New Hutton, 'kill'd by ye Scotts' and one 'Scotch Rebel his name not known', who were buried on the following day.[66]

Perth's party rode northwards to Penrith, but on hearing that further opposition was likely to be found there, tried to avoid the place.[67] However, they were led by their guide into an ambush and came within 'gun-shot range of a great body of both horse and foot' which created panic among the Jacobites. However, they were able to retreat in good order. The countrymen on horseback then pursued them, albeit unsuccessfully, as far as Orton, and their intended prey reached Shap. Possibly one of the Jacobites was taken. At this point, beacons were lit in the immediate vicinity, alerting other countrymen to the presence of the Jacobites, and so Perth's men, fearing a renewed assault, retreated to Kendal, where they met the main body of their army.[68] Yet when the main Jacobite force eventually approached Penrith, the 'great many militia' there left the town.[69]

However, as with the magistrates of Manchester, those of Kendal had to placate an angrier Jacobite army on the following day. Only with great difficulty were they able to pacify the officers, by arguing that the people at the market place who attacked the Jacobites were not Kendal residents but countrymen and so the Kendal inhabitants were innocent of the attack. Cameron of Lochiel accepted this version of events, and after taking the public monies, the town was left at peace, save for a little alleged looting by a few of the Jacobite rear guard.[70]

Some of the irregular loyalist forces which were raised locally were horsemen and numbered between 200 and 300. Whilst marching through Cumberland, the Jacobite Johnstone records 'a great number of the enemy's light-horse continually hovering about us, without venturing, however, to come within musket-shot.' At one stage it appeared as if they were forming into an order of battle, but nothing ever came of this. When threatened, they fled.[71] One contemporary observed 'But they [the Jacobites] kept in so compact a body that we thought the attempt impracticable, especially considering the difference of weapons and numbers', but a few stragglers were rounded up.[72] Parties of countrymen at Keswick and Ireby, initially believed that the Jacobites to be few in number and therefore vulnerable.

[Figure 29] Plaque in Devonshire Street, Penrith; referring to the town's Jacobite links. Photograph by Geoff Wilson (2006).

It is uncertain who the Cumberland and Westmorland men were who were so militant in their opposition to the Jacobites. Although Jarvis discussed the militia of these counties in detail, he did not consider them. They were probably not militia under the command of the lieutenancy because the latter was absentee. A contemporary reference to them states 'there were no officers among them and the people were very ill-arm'd.'[73] However, there was probably some organising force behind them. One letter claimed that the county sheriff (Joshua Lucock of Cockermouth) and his deputy took charge of the men after having summoned them together.[74] Although Lonsdale was absentee, he had contacted the deputy lieutenants and JPs there and they may have assisted in organising the country people. Cumberland himself suggested the sheriff summon the posse.[75] Their endeavours, however, were unsuccessful. Although the men of Appleby planned to attack a group of 20 Jacobites at Thrimby, they learnt that there were actually 500 of them, and so 'thought it proper to retreat, though in very good order' and took eight Jacobite stragglers to Appleby gaol.[76]

But if they could not stop the Jacobites, the magistrates were able to assist the regular army in other ways. On 12 December, Cumberland wrote to the deputy lieutenants of Westmorland to ask if they could break up roads and fell trees across them in order to impede the Jacobites' retreat.[77] Some roads were damaged as requested by Cumberland, on the orders of the Westmorland JPs. The road from Kendal to Shap had been broken. This prevented the four-wheeled ammunition carts from traversing them. New ones had to be constructed but this took time and delayed their march. They also had Wasdale Bridge destroyed.[78] The Westmorland JPs gave 12 horse loads of bread, cheese and ale to them.[79] Whitehaven gentlemen offered to send Cumberland ten eighteen pounder cannon, together with 400 cannon balls, if he needed these. They were to be crucial in effecting a breach in Carlisle's walls.[80] Fawkener passed on Cumberland's satisfaction for their 'repeated marks...of the finest and most considerable zeal'.[81]

[Figure 30] Memorial to 'The Battle of Clifton Moor', 18 December 1745. Photograph by David Oates (2005).

It was at the little village Clifton, just south of Penrith, that the last skirmish between two formed bodies of troops took place on English soil on 18 December. Lord George Murray was in command of the Jacobite rearguard, stationed in the vicinity of the village, whilst the bulk of the army was retreating northwards. The advance guard of Cumberland's army, composed of mounted infantry and cavalry, had at last, reached them.

Murray had four regiments – the Appin Stewarts, Cluny's McPhersons, Glengarry's McDonalds and Roy Stuart's Edinburgh regiment. Although he had requested another 1,000 men from Penrith, none were forthcoming. He posted the troops he had behind hedges to await Cumberland's troops, who advanced in two lines.[82]

The skirmish began as the sun set. After a fire fight between the advancing dragoons, who were dismounted to fight as infantry, Cluny's McPhersons charged, sword in hand. There was no time for another volley and a melee developed. The dragoons were pushed back and the Jacobites were able to retreat unmolested as darkness prevented any further advance by the regulars. Both sides claimed a victory – the regulars because they remained on the field; the Jacobites because their retreat had not been disrupted. Casualties were low on both sides.[83]

The regulars, were, as in Lancashire and Cheshire, welcomed. Thomas Savage, a Quaker, and thus a pacifist, entertained the soldier, Cumberland, after the skirmish at Clifton and later wrote that his guest was 'pleasant agreeable company he was – a man of parts, very friendly and no pride in him'.[84] Thomas Shepherd of Kendal was even more effusive, writing on 24 December:

> The glorious appearance of His Royal Highness the Duke of Cumberland in this Town has left a lasting impression of Joy and Gratitude on the minds of the inhabitants. He made us happy and we know ourselves to be under his courage and conduct: he drove away the Rebells at the very crisis…He dissipated our Fears, animated our Hopes, filled every heart with Joy and every house with festivity…May the God of Battles give safety to His Royal Highness' person, success to his cause. [85]

When erroneous news arrived at Whitehaven that the Jacobite army had been defeated at Lancaster, there were great rejoicings there. Candles and tar barrels were burnt and some gunpowder was lit to mark the occasion.[86] Likewise, the arrival of Cumberland's advance guard at Penrith 'afforded much Satisfaction to the Townspeople', in part because they had been saved

[Figure 31]
Memorial to the fallen Jacobites at Clifton Moor on 18 December 1745. Photograph by David Oates (2005).

IN MEMORY OF THE TROOPERS
OF
'BLANDS REGIMENT'
WHO LIE HERE
KILLED ON CLIFTON MOOR
1745

PRESENTED BY
'THE QUEEN'S
ROYAL HUSSARS'

[Figure 32] Gravestone to the memory of the men of Bland's dragoons slain at Clifton Moor on 18 December 1745. Photograph by David Oates (2005).

from the consequences of their recent hostility to the Jacobite advance guard.[87]

As to the English recruits in the Jacobite army, on realising that retreat meant travelling to Scotland, some took the chance to desert. According to Daniel, by the time they had reached Carlisle 'many had quitted and returned home being unwilling to go to Scotland'.[88] David Morgan, the Welsh attorney from Preston, announced 'By God I had rather be hanged than go to Scotland' and, subsequently, his wish was answered.[89] But many did not. When Perth asked Daniel what he thought of the prospect, he replied 'I had ever been curious to see that Kingdom, and was proud of benefiting the cause on occasion that was offered'. Another Jacobite in the north west who was not downhearted was one Lucy Slater, wife of a publican at Eamont Bridge, who told retreating Jacobites that a local man, Thomas Robinson, had taken part in the harrying of Perth's hussars.[90]

On 19 December, the Jacobite army was at Carlisle and a garrison of about 400 men was left there, including the remnant of the Manchester Regiment, which remained, due to the urgings of Townley. This was despite the wishes of many of his officers and men who desired to stay with the main army and enter Scotland. Yet Townley disregarded these wishes and told them that Charles wished that they would stay at Carlisle. At this point they 'most willingly acquiesced, shewing true English bravery in any situation to obey'. Daniel saluted their courage, observing that these men were 'not of an extraordinary rank', yet they put others of nobler blood to shame.[91]

Cumberland arrived outside Carlisle on 21 December and was given a great deal of help in his siege of Carlisle by the country people, who had not helped the besieging Jacobites in the same fashion in the previous month. Jerome Tullie and Montague Farriers, JPs, wrote warrants which were issued to the constables of Grinsdale, Beaumont and Kirkandrews to

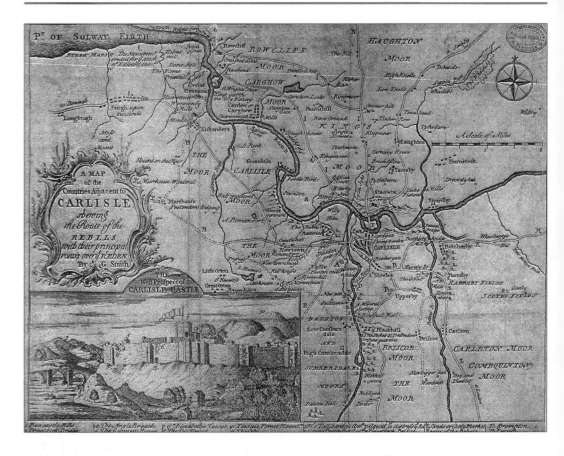

produce horses, carts and 26 men to transport stones from Sandsfield to Carlisle and to take artillery from there to Allonby, 16 miles away. The county officials also provided corn and hay for the army's horses. Inhabitants of Cockermouth brought cannon and balls from there to Carlisle. Over 50 men from Dalston helped erect batteries for the siege. Twenty Weatheral men dug trenches for the besiegers. This was despite being fired upon, albeit ineffectively, by the Jacobite artillery.[92] Of course, all these officials expected to be repaid, and mostly were, but without their efforts, the siege's outcome would certainly have been delayed. Cumberland was also offered the assistance of 'a great many people' armed with clubs and staves, allegedly numbering 10,000. However, he dismissed most of them, except those needed to cut fascines (bundles of wooden faggots used to protect gunners from enemy fire) for the batteries.[93]

Cumberland was also helped by the intrepid men of the Liverpool Blues. They had received orders to march from Chester on 11 December and went northwards, following Cumberland's forces. Reaching Carlisle on 25 December, they formed part of the force which was besieging the Jacobite-held town. Their role in the last siege on English soil was unglamorous but necessary. They stood guard lest any of their enemy made sallies or

[Figure 33]
A Map of the counties adajacent to Carlisle by G. Smith.
The Gentleman's Magazine, XVI, 1746.

[Figure 35]
Opposite: 'Carlisle, from the Duke of Cumberland's batteries, in 1745'. Reproduced by permission of Carlisle Library.

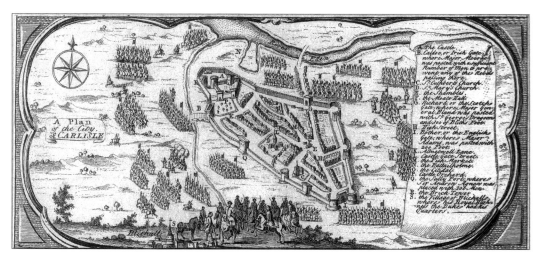

[Figure 34]
'Carlisle invested by
the Duke of
Cumberland, 21st
December 1745'.
Reproduced by
permission of
Carlisle Library.

attempted to escape. Graham was fired upon, but otherwise, the danger
was minimal. It was a relief when the castle and town fell on 30 December
as had there been an assault, some of the Liverpool Blues would have taken
part in it.[94] It is worth noting that the zeal of the Liverpool Blues was
significant – usually county militia would not march outside the borders
of their county and yet these men had marched many leagues to the north
of theirs and had stood alongside the regulars.

The town and castle fell because the heavy guns Cumberland needed to
make a breach in the walls had been provided by the gentlemen of
Whitehaven. The Jacobites surrendered once a breach had been made. The
townspeople had been much concerned about what might happen next and

The Duke of Cumberland — *refusing to treat with the Rebels.*

sought out Townley, hoping to save their lives. They were fortunate, for, though he wished to fight on, he was overruled by Hamilton and the majority of the other officers. Morale among the garrison was also low, with men deserting their posts on the walls and refusing to fight on – shades indeed of the civilian defenders of Carisle in the previous months.[95] Thus ended the last siege on English soil.

There were some who merely observed events and recorded them without any further comment. Such a one was the Rev. Williamson, who only resided a few miles from Carlisle. His first reference to the Jacobites in his diary for December was on the 13th, to note 'An Acct that ye Hgd. Army were returning Northwards'.[96] However, from the 15 to the 31 December almost all of his one line daily entries contains a reference to the topic. Although Williamson was inactive, even his mind was impressed by the siege of Carlisle and the military action thereabouts. [97]

Finally it is worth noting that they were probably many who were very relieved that the invaders had left without doing too much damage. James Clegg wrote in his diary 'Blessed be God that the silk mill is safe'.[98] A similar note of relief was struck by the Rev. George Booth (1707–1764) who wrote ' A sad horrible month in Chester and ye county never to be forgot.'[99]

[Figure 36] 'The Duke of Cumberland refusing to treat with the Rebels', S. Wale del, C. Grignion, sculp. Reproduced by permission of Carlisle Library.

Conclusion

Despite the hopes of senior figures in the Hanoverian elite, the counties had not proved effectual in attempting to halt the fleeing Jacobites in December. This was only partly because Derby had fled from Lancashire, Lonsdale was absentee and the militia in all these counties were disbanded. The whole system which would have worked in times of peace had been completely disrupted by the Jacobite march southwards and so was unable to operate. Even had this not been so, it is just as difficult to see that they could have acted any differently to what they had done in the previous month. Once again it was left to rather informal methods to make even a semblance of resistance at Manchester, but as before, these men had dispersed on hearing that a strong body of formed men was approaching them. It was only at Kendal and Penrith that stiffer resistance was possible, and then only against small groups of Jacobites. Regular troops, though, were greeted with enthusiasm, at Macclesfield, for instance, or more materially helped, for example, during the siege of Carlisle. Irregular forces behaved well in conjunction with the regulars, as at Carlisle. Instances of Jacobitism in the north west at this time were, understandably, rare.

CHAPTER FOUR

1746 and After

In the early months of 1746, with the Jacobite army now in Scotland and the French invasion force stood down, what was to prove the end game was played out in the Highlands and the focus of the campaign moved away from the north west. For the Jacobite army, despite a victory over the regulars, led by General Hawley, at Falkirk on 17 January and a string of lesser successes, lack of money and supplies led to desertions and a weakened force. Cumberland resumed command of the regulars and, well supplied from the sea, inexorably marched towards them. The climax came on Culloden Moor on 16 April and the hitherto invincible Jacobite army was routed with many casualties. This marked the end of the rebellion; Charles eventually escaping to France whilst his followers dispersed.

This meant that activity in the north west was at a lower pitch than in the preceding two months, but it did not mean that the impact of the invasion was at an end. Its consequences were deeply felt over the next few years. For loyalists in the north west there was rejoicing; but for Jacobite sympathisers and captured Jacobites, these were unhappy times. Yet, though the Jacobite venture had been crushed, Jacobitism remained a creed there for some for decades to come.

Generally speaking, at least for some, life carried on as normal after the last two months of hectic activity and alarm. Beppy Byrom enjoyed her busy social life which ranged from tea drinking and gossip to hunting.[1] Although Williamson's life had never been seriously put out by the invasion and subsequent retreat, he could report similar pastimes being enjoyed.[2] Kay began to return to his patients and to 'Domestick Affairs'.[3]

Not all were able to pursue such pastimes untroubled by distant events. Lonsdale commented on the battle of Falkirk, but noted that the Jacobites had been unable to exploit their victory.[4] Derby wrote on 4 April 'I agree in your opinion that the Rebellion is far from being over, and heartily wish England may not again be visited with the same sort of unwelcome guests.'[5] The rebellion was still a controversial topic, as Kay indicated on 15 January 'Times at present run high amongst us; Some shewing themselves much in favour for the present government, and but too many for the Pretender'.[6] Kay remembered the campaign in his prayers and trusted, on 4 February, that God would 'dispose of these great and weighty Affairs for the Good of the Nation'.[7]

Military and Judicial Activity

With the campaign in England over with the fall of Carlisle, the Liverpool Blues marched southwards on 1 January. Their officers saluted Cumberland as he reviewed the force before their departure. They returned to Liverpool on 8 January, where there was thought to be some possibility that they might enter into the regular establishment. However, the turn of the campaign probably biased the government against such a possibility. After a final review on Town Field on 14 January, the men were dismissed, for the subscription money which had financed them was now used up. They had behaved well and acquitted themselves with credit. One of the junior officers, Walter Shairp, remarked with pride 'We were the best New Regiment raised in the Kingdom' and was not a little displeased that the government had taken no further notice of them. Yet he had had an enjoyable time

> During the time that I was engaged in this affair I cant say that I ever before spent any time more agreeably and I am sure that most of the gentlemen that were with us will say the same with me. For though we frequently had a great dale of fatigue & trouble in our marches and other ways yet that was always made more than amends for by the mirth & joy that we afterwards had when we got into our Quarters & the constant Harmony that we lived in with one another.[8]

The Liverpool Blues had been a very effective irregular unit – probably because it was led by regular officers who had the trust of those beneath them and worked in conjunction with the regulars.

The work of the military was over. That of magistrates could now begin. In contrast to their behaviour in the preceding weeks, they were rather more active, now the immediate danger was over, but also because men could reassemble and so it was possible to convene and to question suspects without fear of interruption by the invaders. In Lancashire, in April, John Hatton of Melling, who had make a Jacobite toast in the previous year, was ordered to be taken to Ormskirk and 'severely whipt' and that the Sheriff was to attend such proceedings.[9] Constables were ordered to make lists of Catholics residing in their jurisdictions.[10] On 7 February, three Irish Catholic priests, suspected of collecting money for the Jacobites in the previous year, were committed to Lancaster gaol.[11] One Mr. Kent of Chester was arrested for treasonable conversation with Jacobite prisoners.[12] Another two Jacobites were sent to the Castle by the Cheshire JPs.[13] In February, men were questioned before the JPs in both Manchester and Cheshire to ascertain either their behaviour during the late invasion or that of others.[14]

As might be expected, Hoghton was zealous in rounding up anyone suspected of Jacobitism. He not only continued his pursuit of Charles Douglas, but began to act against the Manchester constables, Rev. Clayton and other Jacobites in the county. He was assisted and encouraged by Newcastle in his activity, and enlisted the support of his fellow JPs. He also helped Henry Masterman, a lawyer working for the Crown against Jacobite prisoners. Those of his colleagues, such as Mr. Kenyon, the Clerk of the Peace, who appeared less enthusiastic to take strong measures against the Catholics, came in for strong condemnation – Hoghton recommending his dismissal.[15]

Officials in the north west who had been accused of sympathising with the Jacobites faced legal action. On 22 April the Manchester constables were taken at Northwich by a party of dragoons and on the following day, Francis Whitlock, a barber, thought to possess treasonable papers, was also taken, but escaped.[16] In June, those Manchester officials were questioned in London 'in order to be try'd for treasonable practices'.[17] Carlisle's mayor, Joseph Backhouse, James Pearson, town clerk, and eight others were taken for having proclaimed Charles as Prince in the preceding year, to much local consternation.[18]

Locally there was much sympathy for these men. Lowther wrote on 11 February of 'the unreasonable charge and trouble the mayor and town clerk of Carlisle have bin putt to by the misrepresentation of some ill designing people'.[19] In February, petitions were sent to attest the loyalty of the Carlisle aldermen. Their fellows, and the local clergy, sent a petition to state that Backhouse and Pattinson were well affected.[20] The aldermen were examined, but the evidence was that they had been forced to behave in such a manner and, this, along with their earlier good behaviour towards King George, resulted in there being insufficient evidence for a prosecution.[21] Eventually all these officials were released, to much rejoicing in the north west. When one of the Manchester constables, Walley, was released, untried, in August 1746, the town's bells were rung to welcome him back. When his colleague, Fowden, was released after being cleared of all charges at the Lancashire Assizes in 1747, church bells rang in Manchester and there were other public rejoicings, by both those who saw him as a loyal subject of George II and were glad to see him vindicated, and by Jacobites who presumably saw him as one of their own.[22] Excuses were made in towns suspected of Jacobitism; in Manchester, it was claimed that only a few men of 'abandoned principles and desperate Fortunes' had joined the Jacobites and thus it was unfair that 'Our Town should be stigmatised with Disloyalty which opprobus Character we are far from deserving'.[23]

Other matters were dealt with by the county Quarter Sessions. Money was spent on transporting the army's baggage northwards, to the tune of at least £200.[24] Bridges damaged by the Liverpool Blues had to be repaired; Warrington bridge cost the county of Lancashire £114 15s 8d, for instance, in material and labour.[25] Payment was also made by the Cheshire JPs to repair the Warrington bridge, too, 'for the immediate Benefit and service to the Publick'. They also spent £40 10s 6d to repair Frodsham bridge.[26]

Officials were also eager to claim what expenses they could after the costs to which they had been put. Chester Corporation made a petition in November 1746 to the Lords of the Treasury for the 'considerable sums of money expended by the city during the late unnaturall rebellion'.[27] Money for replacing stones taken from the churchyard to repair defences was repaid in May 1748.[28]

The Easter Quarter Sessions of the county of Cumberland were inundated with petitions for recompense. These were mostly from high constables and other officials who had expended money in procuring horses and carts to move army baggage, wounded soldiers or Jacobite prisoners in the previous December and January. These petitions continued to be heard until Easter 1748. It is not clear whether all these men were reimbursed. Some were – the inhabitants of Great Salkeld received £1 16s at the Michaelmass Sessions in 1746 for moving military baggage from Penrith to Kendal, but others did not, and there are notes reading 'Nil' against some of the petitions. Some payments were delayed.[29]

From January 1746, Jacobite prisoners were distributed in several castles and prisons throughout the north west. In February, there were 165 in Lancaster, 116 in Chester, 25 in Whitehaven, whilst French prisoners were held in Penrith, as well as many being held in Carlisle.[30] Treason trials were held in Carlisle in September, beginning on 9 September. They were concluded 20 days later. A total of 127 men had been tried and 91 had been found guilty and sentenced to death. It is interesting to note that some claimed that they were not Jacobites and were forced into their ranks.[31] Most of these men were Scots, brought to Carlisle after Culloden, but a few were from the north west – though most of the latter, especially the officers, were tried in London. Those in Carlisle included the Coppock brothers, John Rowbotham, Philip Hunt and Thomas Turner. Thomas Coppock and six others tried to escape by secretly sawing off their chains, but the attempt was detected.[32] Nine, included Thomas Coppock, were executed at Carlisle on 18 October and another nine died at Brampton three days later. On the same day, nine more were hanged at Penrith.[33] On 15 December, the last ten executions took place at Carlisle.[34] Others tried but not executed were either acquitted (36), transported (15) or enlisted into the army in order to gain a pardon (21). Five were pardoned outright, four died in gaol and one man turned King's evidence. Those not tried were mostly transported. The officers of the Manchester Regiment were mostly tried in London, and of 23, ten were hanged and three transported.[35]

It is uncertain what local opinion thought of these trials and subsequent executions. Peploe wrote to Newcastle on 14 July to state his views 'I hope some examples will be made at Manchester of this detestable Rebellion

where some particular persons are as insolent as ever'.[36] Of course, Peploe had had his own issues with some of the Manchester clergy in the past, so had an additional axe to grind. A rather different view was expressed, or rather not, by Williamson. He noted laconically that the judges were at Carlisle in September and that nine of the Jacobite prisoners were hanged there on 18 October, but no more.[37] Jacobite propaganda was circulated in Carlisle at the time of the trials and this may have disposed locals to favour the Jacobites. Yet there is no recorded support for their cause there. However, in Manchester, Beppy Byrom referred to 'poor Bobby Deacon' and one Manchester woman took almost £4 worth of food for the prisoners.[38] Sympathy for the prisoners could come from unexpected quarters. Thomas Brereton, a Whig MP for Liverpool, petitioned for mercy for Thomas Furnivall, arguing he was 'a very weak man and consequently the more easily seduced and hurried into rebellion by bad company'. He was eventually released in 1749.[39]

The money motive was on the mind of Richard Gildart, alderman of Liverpool. On 18 September 1746 he and one Samuel Smith of London were awarded the contract to transport Jacobite prisoners to the American colonies. Hoping for £5 10s per prisoner, the treasury gave them £5. By 26 May 1747 Gildart had shipped 157 prisoners from Liverpool to the American colonies.[40]

Perhaps a more surprising prisoner was Dr. Bracken, thrown into Lancaster Castle in January 1746 by his enemies; perhaps disgruntled Tories

[Figure 37]
'Execution of Rebels at Carlisle', 1746. Reproduced by permission of Carlisle Library.

and Jacobites who found his loyalism of the previous year sickening. He was later released and became Mayor of Lancaster in the following year.[41]

Demonstrations of Loyalty

There were a number of loyalist celebrations throughout the country in 1746. These were, in early January, the fall of Carlisle, in April to celebrate both Cumberland's birthday on 15 April and his victory at Culloden; then finally on 9 October which was appointed by the government as a day of national thanksgiving for the defeat of the rebellion. Many of these celebrations had religious overtones, which is understandable as many Anglicans and most Dissenters were virulently opposed to the Popery espoused by the Jacobite cause.

On 3 January, with the news that Carlisle had fallen to the regulars, there were celebrations in Manchester. Bells rang, buildings were lit up and an effigy of Charles Stuart was shot at, quartered and then burnt. These demonstrations were led by the Dissenters and they encouraged others by giving them drinks. The only dissident was the Jacobite Rev. Cattell, who refused to have his house illuminated.[42] The townsmen only wished that Cumberland might pass through there on his way southwards so they could show their appreciation of his valour.[43] Mr. Bayley of Manchester wrote to tell the good news to his friend, James Clegg of Derbyshire, who was in receipt of this on 4 January.[44] Parishes rang their bells to celebrate; in Lancashire, those of Ribchester rang 'when News came of the Rebels being subdued at Carlisle' and at Maghull, money was spent 'upon ye Ringers when Carlisle surrendered'.[45]

Rejoicing did not always go as planned. On 22 January, there was a report in Manchester that Hawley had beaten the Jacobite army at Falkirk. The Presbyterians sent a messenger to ascertain this and on the following day 'they have ordered the bells to be ready to ring and say there shall be such rejoicing as never was in Manchester'. They were to be disappointed when the truth was discovered.[46]

In Blackburn, Cumberland's birthday was celebrated on 15 April. There were great rejoicings by bells being rung, bonfires lit and houses lit up. An effigy of the crowd's hero was carried through the town 'with great splendour' and there was also an effigy of a highlander with a noose around his neck.[47] Likewise, at Penrith, there was, on this occasion, 'the most signal demonstrations of Joy'.[48] In Cheshire, Stockport's bells rang, as did those of St. John's, Chester, but many did not.[49]

Once the news of the battle of Culloden came, loyalists could rejoice again. Derby reported on 2 May 'I most heartily rejoice with you for His Royal Highness' success in Scotland'.[50] On 27 April there was a thanksgiving service held at Bury chapel, and God was praised for the victory. There was another such event on the following Sunday once definite news had arrived.[51]

The city of Carlisle spent money on ale and bonfires for a number of loyalist events throughout 1746 – on Cumberland's birthday, on 24 April to celebrate the victory at Culloden and on 11 June, the anniversary of the King's accession. On 24 April, ten gallons of ale was supplied to the townspeople and 9s 6d was spent on fire and candles.[52] In Chester, £7 2s was spent on post-Culloden celebrations.[53]

Churches throughout the counties rang their bells to celebrate these events. In Cumberland and Westmorland, the parish of Heversham gave five shillings to the bell ringers for ringing on 'Rejoicing Days for defeating Rebels', and the same payment was made at Greystoke on two different occasions, one being 'upon the Victory over the Rebels in Scotland'.[54] At Beetham three shillings was given for bell ringing on Cumberland's birthday. A similar payment was made at Hawkshead, where five shillings was spent on this occasion, including ale for the bell ringers.[55] The day nationally appointed for such celebrations was marked in Morland by bell ringing.[56] The accounts of Penrith merely refer to the ringers being paid on unspecified, but surely similar, rejoicing days'.[57] In Lancashire, the story was the same. At Kirkham, the bells rang for two days and one night 'at News of the Duke's victory' and twelve shillings were thus expended. On a slightly different footing, money was 'spent at old Barstow's when ye reports of ye rebels being beat at Maghull were heard.[58]

There were also secular displays of joy. On 30 April, Kay recorded that he had 'spent the Evening here with some Neighbouring Friends in

[Figure 38]
Duke of Cumberland Inn, Farleton, Westmorland. By Atkinson & Pollitt, publishers of The Westmorland Gazette, c.1925. Reproduced courtesy of Holme and District Local History Society.

rejoicing at the good News from Scotland'.[59] At Preston, the news was 'received here with all those Transports of Joy, that could arise in the hearts of a people sensible of so signal a Blessing'. There was a great procession through the town of people of both sexes and 'of all Ages and Ranks'. The mayor and the corporation, the town's trades companies, volunteers and others paraded with colours flying and drums beating. There were loyal toasts and a ball; each street allegedly had its own bonfire.[60] All wished to be associated with the victory.

Similarly, in Manchester, bonfires were made, bells rung and houses were illuminated. Whig clergymen and gentry met at The Angel and drank loyal toasts, and gave ale to the populace to do likewise. Great numbers put on cockades to express their joy in public. Yet the local newspaper hinted at a lack of unanimity 'On all Occasions, especially such as these, it were heartily to be wish'd there were no other Distinctions amongst us but those of Friends or Enemies to the present Government'.[61] In fact, in September, it was noted 'We have had some of Bland's dragoons here near a fortnight, and now our people begin to be a little quieter'.[62] Lord Malpas thought that the soldiers 'frightened them into rejoicing'.[63]

Loyal addresses were sent. The first to send them were the corporations of Chester and Liverpool in late May. The latter's was glowing indeed, 'testifying the unfeigned joy we feel on the success of your Majesty's Arms in Scotland'. It went on to refer to Culloden as 'This glorious Event' and that the Jacobites had met with their 'just punishment'. They referred to 'the unfeigned Joy we feel on the success of your Majesty's Arms in Scotland'. They also hoped that this 'will establish the throne of this kingdom more firmly in your Majesty's illustrious House'.[64] Penrith and Whitehaven sent theirs later in the month; with Lancaster and Westmorland sending theirs in June. Last of all was the county of Cumberland in late July. These loyal addresses also praised Duke of Cumberland, glorified the status quo and the blessings of George II's rule. They also scourged the defeated Jacobites and referred to the alleged evils of a successful rebellion – the loss of religion, liberty, laws and property.[65] A sermon which was very much of its time was made by the Rev. William Smith, Rector of Holy Trinity, Lancaster, in July 1746. Smith made anti-Catholic remarks, linking Catholicism with absolutism in Europe and with the reign of James II; the people of England being saved by both by the forces of Protestantism, and liberty.[66]

October 9 was marked by both Anglican and Dissenting clergy. Mr. Braddock preached at Bury chapel on this occasion.[67] While we do not know the content of his oration, those of Anglican clergy and Dissenting ones were very similar to one another. Those by two Lancashire clergymen, the forementioned Maddox and the Dissenting Josiah Owen of Rochdale, a friend of Kay's, have survived.[68] They both spent much time on the terrors of a French and Catholic yoke that Jacobite success would have wrought.[69]

The Duke of Cumberland was praised as a heroic deliverer; Maddox claiming 'We can never sufficiently admire and praise the unparalleled Bravery and conduct of His Royal Highness the Duke of Cumberland'.[70] His father, the King, was also lauded 'long may he adorn' the throne, proposed Owen.[71] Maddox also urged his congregation to lead better lives and praise God for His mercy.[72]

In Chester, the thanksgiving day was met with a similar expenditure. Waits (street singers) were hired at ten shillings to provide musical entertainment; tobacco and pipes at four shillings, biscuits at four shillings, candles at six shillings and wine at £5 16s. The bell ringers were also paid to ring on the occasion.[73]

Such celebrations continued in October, at least in Manchester. There was ball on 30 October, to mark the King's 63rd birthday, but it was also as a benefit concert to a dancing master who had lost much business on account of his loyalty to the government in the previous year. Apparently, 'there was a Numerous Assembly of Loyalists, the Evening was spent with Musick and Dancing and Singing the Song of, God save great George our King'.[74] Toasts were made to the King, the Prince and Princess of Wales, Cumberland, the army and to the late William III. Although the clergy of the Collegiate Church attended, some gentry and clergymen did not.

[Figure 39]
One of two brass chandeliers hanging in the nave of St. Andrew's Church, Penrith. These were given to the townspeople by the Duke of Portland for their loyalty during the invasion. Photograph by Geoff Wilson (2006). Reproduced by permission of Penrith Parochial Church Council.

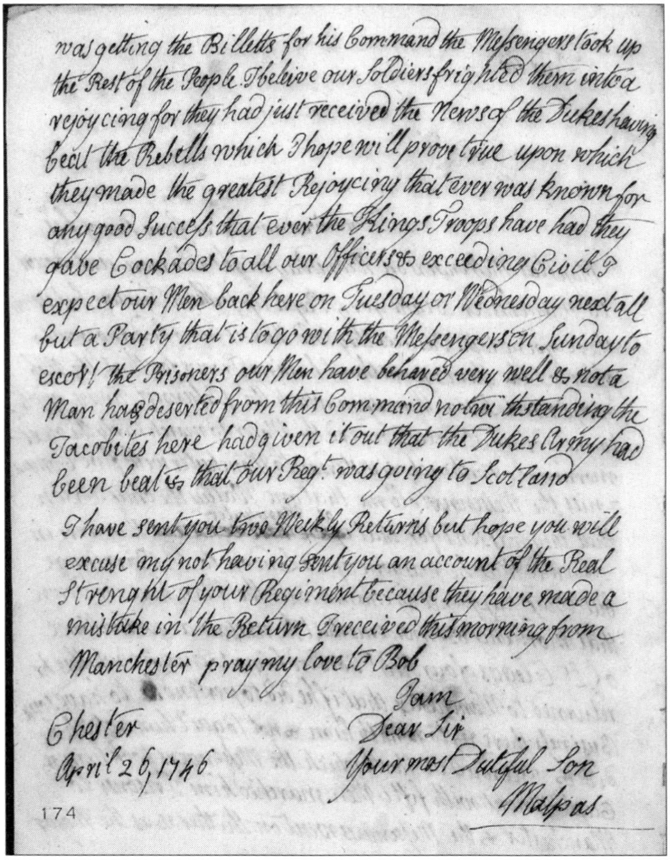

was getting the Billets for his Command the Messengers took up the Rest of the People I believe our Soldiers frighted them into a rejoycing for they had just received the News of the Dukes having beat the Rebells which I hope will prove true upon which they made the greatest Rejoycing that ever was known for any good Success that ever the Kings Troops have had they gabe Cockades to all our Officers & exceeding Civil I expect our Men back here on Tuesday or Wednesday next all but a Party that is to go with the Messengers on Sunday to escort the Prisoners our Men have behaved very well & not a Man has deserted from this Command notwithstanding the Jacobites here had given it out that the Dukes Army had been beat & that our Reg.t was going to Scotland

I have sent you two Weekly Returns but hope you will excuse my not having sent you an account of the Real Strenght of your Regiment because they have made a mistake in the Return I received this morning from Manchester pray my love to Bob

Chester
April 26, 1746
174

I am
Dear Sir
Your most Dutiful Son
Malpas

[Figure 40]
Lord Malpas suggests loyalist rejoicing in Chester in April 1746 is due to presence of regular soldiers. Reproduced by permission of The National Archives. TNA, SP36/83, f175v.

The Manchester Magazine took to printing a great deal of anti-Jacobite material. In January there was a long piece belittling Charles' claim to the throne; 'the Pretended Son of the Pretender'.[75] The Jacobites were castigated as 'such filthy, farting, shitting…' Scots. Cumberland's efforts were praised thus 'the indefatigable pains of his Royal Highness'. The defeat of the regular army under Hawley at Falkirk was played down.[76] The Scots were castigated as being cannibals.[77] It also advertised John Marchant's *History of the Present Rebellion*, soon to be on sale, trying to catch local custom by claiming to include 'A Curious Plan' of Manchester.[78]

The following year saw similar events. There was a ball at the Manchester Exchange on 15 April 1747 to celebrate Cumberland's birthday, with tickets at two shillings each.[79] On 21 April 1747, a ball was held in Manchester to celebrate the first anniversary of the victory at Culloden. It was opened by Samuel Birch, the county's High Sheriff and Lady Hoghton was also present. Apparently it was patronised by 'a most brilliant Appearance of Gentlemen and Ladies'.[80]

Kay recalled the rebellion from the vantage point of 1747 and 1748. In November 1747, when commenting on a current struggle between the High Church and his own Presbyterians, he likened the former to 'the evil spirit' which had been abroad during the rebellion. As for Culloden, he wrote 'Blessed be God for the happy Defeat of the Rebells'.[81] On 16 April 1748 he recalled the second anniversary of the battle with approval.[82]

The heads of Syddall and one of Dr. Deacon's sons, officers in the Manchester regiment, were fixed upon the Exchange at Manchester in October. Kay thought that this set a good example to the public. Kay and his ilk had no sympathy for them, recalling that they were part of a 'wicked, hellish and unaccountable Crew' who had threatened to deprive them of their religious liberty.[83] The windows of houses where the inhabitants celebrated the victory were illuminated; unsurprisingly Sydall's widow did not share in this joy, when her windows were broken by soldiers, the town's magistrates and constables did not intervene.[84]

There were also other violent loyalist responses. These were probably initiated by a violent sermon of one Rev. John Brekell.[85] In Liverpool on 30 April 'a very great and formidable mob of people assembled together before the houses wherein the Romish chapel was kept in the town and immediately began to demolish it'. The mob comprised of sailors and carpenters. The chapel was torn to pieces and the furniture was burnt. Although the magistrates were probably unsympathetic towards Catholicism, they did try to stop the riot and have the perpetrators arrested, but to no effect: the crowd was too strong. On 20 May, the mob destroyed a Liverpool Catholic's house which housed a chapel.[86] Ormskirk chapel was also attacked shortly afterwards and the priest's property was burnt; Catholics being identified with the hated Jacobites.[87] Another violent outbreak of loyalty occurred in Penrith in May 1747, when a French officer, held as a prisoner of war, was pelted with stones and filth. The house of the Jacobite Rev. Daniel was sacked after he fled.[88]

Soldiers generally received a warm welcome from residents – though not always. A female publican at Whitehaven sent Cumberland, when at Carlisle, beer, which he accepted with thanks.[89] At Nantwich, the men of Halifax's regiment were welcomed into the houses of gentlemen and merchants.[90] Yet soldiers in residence for any length of time were unpopular. A petition was sent to the MPs for Lancaster to complain about the two regiments quartered in Manchester and Salford, who had been demanding, unreasonable and threatening towards householders.[91]

[Figure 41]
Mayor of Liverpool describes anti-Catholic rioting in April 1746. Reproduced by permission of The National Archives. TNA, SP36/83, f341r.

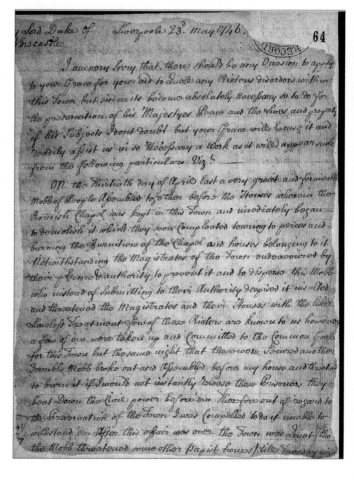

The Survival of Jacobitism

This orgy of congratulation and self satisfaction did not mean that Jacobitism was wholly overwhelmed – certainly not in its Lancashire heartlands, though caution and circumspection were often necessary. After the news of Culloden had been heard, for example, Kay recorded that High Church men and Catholics had appeared to be very disappointed. He also added that in December 1746, they acted against Mr. Crompton, a Presbyterian schoolmaster. He added 'we see a great many disappointed in the glorious Victory at Culloden Moor last spring by the brave Duke of Cumberland'. In the previous month, Kay had been accused of assaulting a lad in the street and attributed this claim to 'Jacobite Wit and Malice'. He prayed for more loyalism and less Jacobitism.[92] Dr. Deacon publicly revered his dead son by bowing and removing his hat each time he passed his head on the spike and it was alleged that he came with a number of others to do so.[93] Some claimed these heads were 'revered, and almost adored, as trophies of martyrdom'.[94]

A number of Lancashire men continued to salute James Stuart in public throughout 1746 and 1747. Jeffrey Battersby of Bury, shoemaker, on 26 April, said 'King George had no right to the Crown of England but that it belonged to the Stuart's family and that no Hanoverian had any right to the throne of England'. He then drank James' health.[95] Two months later, Richard Waring of Chipping, flax dresser, said, at Preston, 'God damn the Duke and the King too. The Duke is a heretick'. Not all accusations of Jacobitism were genuine. Robert Wood accused James Smethurst of a like offence, but it seemed Wood was lying.[96] The authorities took all this very seriously; James Platt of Orford, a whistler, who made similar comments in 1747 was deemed 'to Disquiet and Disturb and discord…to cause sedition and Rebellion'.[97]

There were other examples of Jacobitism in Lancashire in the years after 1745 which involved several people. On 29 May (the anniversary of Charles II's Restoration) 1746, there was a clash between Jacobites and soldiers, in which the latter were singing Cumberland's praises. They were pelted with stones by the Jacobites who sung 'The King Shall enjoy his own again'.[98] In the autumn of 1746 there was a report that the cries of 'Down with the rump [an allusion to the short lived and unpopular republican government prior to the restoration of Charles II in 1660], Down with the Hanoverians, Presbyterians, Down with the King' were common in Manchester.[99] It was claimed that 'Jacobite, nonjuring and even popish principles are now making a greater progress here than ever, being propagated with equal industry and success'.[100] During the loyalist ball in Manchester, a stone was thrown through the window, presumably by a Jacobite.[101] Evelyn Franke, Esq. of Preston was alleged to have shouted 'Down with the Rump' and then to have assembled a mob in order to disturb the peace and attempted riot.[102] George Robinson of Chester, in 1746, was accused of 'a high crime and misdemeanour by which he gave great offence to many of His Majesty's good subjects'.[103]

In 1747, there was a clash in Rochdale between two mobs at the annual rushbearing. The Blacks were Whiggish and were opposing the Jacks (Jacobites). One Mr. Robinson's house was thought to harbour Jacks and this was attacked by the Blacks, who were joined by some soldiers. Plaid handkerchiefs were hanging out of the windows and the contents of chamber pots were hurled at their assailants, who in their turn sang a song in praise of the Duke of Cumberland.[104]

There was debate over the apparent Jacobitism in Manchester. One writer alleged it was a fabrication made out of exaggerated reports. He claimed that the Jacobite cries were merely the shouting of drunkards reeling home from the ale house after a discussion on religion and politics. Manchester was said to be merely home to few Catholics and non jurors. Dr. Deacon was allegedly held in high favour by the local clergy and that the heads of the executed Jacobites were not revered by anyone excepting Deacon who had saluted his son's once.[105]

Another point of view was made by one 'Philopatriae'. This was that this counter argument was merely a smokescreen for Jacobite behaviour in Manchester, 'calculated to bring those strange times afresh on the stage, by cherishing the seeds of disaffection to the present government'. He claimed that the apologist must be deaf to signs of Jacobitism in Manchester or else blinded by Jacobite prejudice. He thought that numbers of the town's Catholic and non jurors were played down for the same reason.[106] Another commentator had similar views, suggesting that any Catholics were too many, that a reference to the 'rump' in any

[Figure 42]
Photograph of Jacobite glassware numbers 1–3, belonging to the Jacobite Lyme family of Cheshire. The white rose was the Jacobite symbol. Photography by Peter Lole. Reproduced by permission of the National Trust, Lyme Park, Newton Collection.

circumstances was Jacobite inspired and that Deacon's applause was worthy of punishment.[107]

The final word in this debate came in 1747 when the first Tory writer returned to the fray. He charged 'Philiopatriae' with 'false reasoning, partiality, bitterness and fury'. He said that his opponent was biased towards Dissent and antagonistic towards the Anglican Church, likening it to Catholicism. The abuse of Dr. Deacon was roundly condemned as being based on falsehoods.[108]

Jacobitism in Manchester remained strong, at least in 1746 and 1747. On Cumberland's birthday in 1746, Jacobites attacked those with cockades in their hats and others who were rejoicing.[109] Stuart and Jacobite symbolism was thick on the ground. On 29 May [Charles II's Restoration Day] 1747, 'The 29th of May/Was sure a happy day/When the King enjoy'd his own again' was sung on the town's streets. Houses of Jacobites were decorated with oak leaves. The 10 June, birthday of James Francis Stuart, was also celebrated there that year. Men wore plaids and ladies had pin cushions marked 'PC'. Toasts were made to 'Church and King' but without naming the latter. When Cumberland was defeated in battle on the Continent in 1747 and when Rev. Clayton was released in the same year, there were celebrations.[110] There were balls in the town in 1749 and 1750, to which only Tories were invited and soldiers excluded. Allegedly, the cries of 'Down with the Rump' and 'Sir Watkin's Jig' were heard from the assembly rooms. This dance was named after Sir Watkin Williams Wynn, a leading Welsh Jacobite.[111]

At Newton, Cheshire, between 20 and 24 November 1748, it was alleged that a meeting of Jacobite gentry occurred, known as the Newton Hunt. James III was proclaimed at the market cross by the gathered throng, who

[Figure 43] Photograph of Jacobite glassware numbered 4–6, belonging to the Jacobite Lyme family of Cheshire. Note the use of the word 'fiat'; Latin for 'Let it be done', referring to a hoped for second Stuart restoration. Photography by Peter Lole. Reproduced by permission of the National Trust, Lyme Park, Newton Collection.

wore white cockades and plaid waistcoats, whilst drinking healths to James Francis Stuart.[112] Yet others claimed that this was merely a private meeting of a hunting party in which there was not the least whiff of sedition.[113] The last seditious words known to have been spoken in public in the county were during an invasion scare of 1757, whilst there was a riot in Preston in 1768 when the cries 'Down with the Rump' and 'No King George' were heard, though the latter might have been a Radical/Wilkesite cry, as Jacobite rhetoric was merged into a newer form of protest.[114]

But much Jacobitism was, as it always had been, in private. A christening dinner in Manchester in 1748 featured images of Charles Stuart in the centre of sweetmeats and the Hanoverians surrounded by chickens and blood oranges.[115] The Byroms had a teapot inscribed with the White Rose and the Mosleys a snuff box with 'Down with the Rump' inscribed. Charles Lawson, headmaster of Manchester Grammar School from 1764 to 1807 was said to be a Jacobite, too.[116] Byrom continued to mark Jacobite anniversaries in private. He wrote to a friend in 1748, thus 'Your 10th of June I supposed passed quietly' and in a letter addressed to his daughter that year, wrote the date thus 'Prince Charles' birthday'.[117] Pro-Stuart drinking clubs were maintained. The corporation of Walton le Dale carried on until 1768 and another one was formed at Ardwick in 1746. Indeed, eight Jacobite clubs were founded in Lancashire and four in Cheshire after 1745. Yet it is unlikely that these posed any threat to the status quo, as far as is known. Most were convivial gatherings in which a toast was occasionally made to the Stuarts.[118]

In the early years of George III's reign, there were a few instances of Jacobitism in Lancashire and Cheshire. Byrom's brother in law, John Houghton, refused the post of county sheriff in 1761 because he would not swear the oath as required, though he was 'a good Protestant and a loyal subject', because he 'had inviolable scruples against the Abjuration Oath'.[119] When Samuel Curwen visited Manchester in 1777, he resided with a Quaker woman, who was 'a Jacobite in political principle', though he noted 'the numbers of which since the English born prince [George III] has mounted the throne is somewhat lessened here'. Yet his hostess and her friends drank Charles' health and hoped for his family's restoration. The men of the house were firm Jacobites, but would do nothing about it. [120]

Horace Walpole made cynical comments about such Jacobites when he wrote, in the 1750s that:

'if the Pretender had succeeded, they could have produced many witnesses to testify their zeal for him; [yet] so cautious that no witnesses of actual; treason could be produced by the government against them: the very sort of Jacobitism that has kept its cause alive, *and kept it from succeeding*'. [121]

Q.E.D.

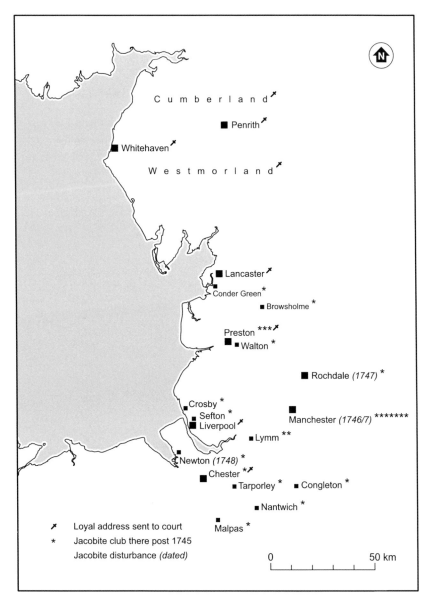

[Map 5]
Map showing loyalist and Jacobite sympathies in the North West of England after Culloden. Map drawn by Simon Chew.

Conclusion

Activity in the north west concerning the Jacobite rebellion of 1745 was at a lower level once the immediate prospect was over and military operations were confined to Scotland once more. The judicial process was put into motion against Jacobite suspects and those thought to have co-operated with them. Most of the latter, though, were found to have been innocent. The defeat of the rebellion was met with an orgy of celebration throughout the north west between 1746 and 1747, but perhaps particularly so in

Lancashire, where the political conflict between Whigs, Dissenters, Tories and non jurors was at its highest. No doubt some was genuine, some mixed with hopes of self advancement. Yet Jacobitism survived; in the hour of apparent defeat, there were men who would proclaim the cause in public and, more commonly, in private, until well into the reign of George III. It would never pose a practical threat to the Hanoverian dynasty, but did indicate that there were some for whom that dynasty would never be accepted as de jure.

Conclusion

The responses of the people of the north west of England to the Jacobite invasion of 1745 were many and varying, and of all hues. It is difficult to draw any hard and fast conclusions because of the lack of evidence about the true motivations behind the actions that we know of. Even the evidence we do have is partial and possibly far from being representative. The conclusions below are therefore, tentative. It is hoped, however, to show that the responses in these counties were varied and not subject to sweeping generalisations, which have often been their lot in the past.

It would appear that the bulk of officialdom, from the Lords Lieutenant to the parish constables, were loyal towards the Hanoverian dynasty. This can be seen in a number of ways. In September and October, loyal addresses were sent to the King, protesting their abhorrence of the Jacobites. The anniversaries of the birthday and Coronation of George II were publicly celebrated, as was 5 November. The militia was called out in Lancashire, Cumberland and Westmorland, volunteers were raised in Liverpool, Carlisle, Penrith, and, in Cheshire, Cholmondeley raised a regiment. A watch was kept on Catholics, there had been some searches and a few arrests, but to a far lesser degree than in 1715, when Cumbrian Catholics had been gaoled. The Church preached against the Jacobites and in favour of the status quo. They acted and reacted; they were not apathetic as they could have been towards a government and King they had severe reservations about, or against a cause they did not find abhorrent.

Yet when the Jacobites invaded these counties, the responses of the volunteers, militia and officials was either to flee, surrender or even proclaim James Stuart as James III. Others assisted the Jacobite effort in handing over public money or facilitating them in other ways. This has often been interpreted as cowardice or evidence of their lack of loyalty to the Hanoverian cause. Yet it would seem that this is, rather, evidence of the fact that, when facing an army of about 5,000 men, far smaller bodies of civilians are almost powerless. Because men do not indulge in suicidal heroics does not mean that they are necessarily craven or lacking in devotion to a cause. Had numbers of regular troops been acting in conjunction with them, the story would probably have been far different – the Liverpool Blues helped the regulars in the siege of Carlisle, for instance. Inability to oppose the enemy was the issue, not disinclination. Whether the flight of civilians was cowardly is another question – but for civilians to flee before an invader, especially one believed to be barbarous and rapacious, is hardly unique to those who did so in north west England in 1745.

Yet there were some in the north west who did act against the Jacobites on their march south to possible victory. Dr. Bracken, Waugh, postmasters and others sent intelligence of the Jacobites to London. Stragglers were captured. The Liverpool Blues wrecked bridges across the Mersey. Small parties of Jacobites were attacked, and successfully so, as at Lowther Hall and at Ormskirk during November 1745.

How far was their rather more militant behaviour on the Jacobite retreat opportunistic? There is no evidence that it was, but rather that it continued the trends which were evident in November and have just been noted. Jacobites were to be attacked wherever possible, which was when their numbers were small. That Cumberland's forces were nearby was a spur, as was the fact that the Jacobites' hitherto exemplary behaviour as regards property, was no longer upheld in December. Likewise, the rejoicing in 1746 following the defeat of the rebellion was following this trend, rather than a mere opportunistic hailing the victor.

The involvement in and sympathy for Jacobitism in the north west was another matter and one, which, in the nature of all underground political movements, especially those which are ultimately unsuccessful, will never be fully known. It is tempting to consider the known strength of Jacobitism with that of Hanoverianism, but to do so requires caution. It took courage to proclaim one's Jacobitism when it was deemed a seditious offence and the punishment for such could be a whipping, a fine or time spent in prison.

Before the Jacobite incursion, evidence for Jacobitism in the north west was virtually nil. Yet in November, the auspices were particularly favourable. This was partly because of the proximity of the Jacobite army. It was then relatively easy to enlist or to show support in other ways, as the means to prevent this were defunct. It should also be recalled that this army had been militarily successful over a body of regular troops in the way that their predecessors in 1715 had not. Many may have believed that the second restoration was imminent, and likened the Jacobite army to that of Monk's in 1660 and concluded a bloodless coup was in the offing, or at least that the regulars would be defeated as they had been at Prestonpans. Death and defeat were not inevitable, despite the results of the two earlier rebellions.

For all that, enlistment was disappointing. In 1685, several thousand Englishmen joined Monmouth. In 1715, at least 426, and probably several hundreds more, from the north west joined Forster's army. The Manchester Regiment numbered between 200 and 300 men and many of these were not from the north west. It was a low number by both contemporary standards and the favourable scenario which has been outlined above. It was only in Lancashire that active Jacobitism was in any ways significant;

in Cheshire, Cumberland and Westmorland it was almost non-existent. The Jacobites of the north west were wholly drawn from the middling sort and common people; unlike 1715, gentry involvement was almost completely absent.

The question to ask is why, if the auspices seemed so favourable and as there was no one to stop anyone showing Jacobite sympathy, so few chose to do so. This cannot be answered with any degree of certainty because there is no evidence to explain why men did not act in the support of the Jacobites. Since correspondence could be intercepted and papers seized, it would be dangerous to betray such reasons to paper.

We are in the realm of possibility, but it is worth advancing a few general hypotheses. First of all, it is highly probable that the failure of the Fifteen, leading as it did to the imprisonment and, sometimes, transportation and death, of those active Jacobites, acted as a powerful disincentive. Secondly, the lack of a foreign army acting alongside the Jacobites may have deterred some; the fact that the Jacobite army was almost wholly Scottish was probably unattractive to most Englishmen. Thirdly, the majority of the English had no military experience and even if they wanted to join, there was a lack of weaponry to arm them and little time to train them. Furthermore, a contemporary historian, hostile to the Jacobites, may have been right when he wrote, recalling the earlier rebellion:

> Upon the Whole, it may be said of the *English Jacobites*, no People in the Universe know better the Difference between drinking and fighting: It is true, the latter they know not practically...Would toasting Healths...reduce Kingdoms, mighty Feats would have been perform'd by the Power of the Bottle and the Glass. [1]

Some Jacobites, such as John Byrom, seemed quite fearful of the Jacobite army and all it implied, though sympathetic to the idea of Jacobitism itself, so preferred passivity to action. Finally, as the gentry did not support the Jacobites, their servants and tenants would not have ventured out, as they did in 1715. In any case, working or professional men with family responsibilities, and lacking any military culture, probably thought it wisest to remain at home and not risk life and limb. English Jacobites, as with their Whig equivalents in 1688, were not fanatical and bloody revolutionaries, but essentially moderate and conservative.

Support for armed action on behalf of Jacobitism was limited. But it was, as a political/religious/social movement, remarkably resilient. Military defeat in 1746 did not crush the spirit of its followers in its Lancashire, and especially Mancunian, heartland. Whether in private or in public, the flame died hard, though its political significance diminished over time. It is important to note that English Jacobitism was largely a social and political phenomenon, not a military one. It was always unlikely that they would be able to give the Jacobite army the kind of support it desired and needed if it were to succeed.

The 'negative' impact of the behaviour of the Jacobites of the north west was to help persuade the Jacobite council that the army should retreat at Derby, or at least to give the pessimists seemingly valid reasons for that action. More Jacobite support would not have made the army much stronger in military terms, but it would have provided an invaluable psychological crutch to those such as Charles Stuart, who had claimed all along that mass support in England existed. As far as the wider campaign went, the importance of the north west lay in what did not happen. It was the dog which, in a Sherlock Holmes story, did not bark in the night time.

As we have seen, the men and women of the north western counties acted in a variety of ways to the Jacobite invasion of 1745. Most were not heroes, but there was little opportunity for them to be so. In the military scenario into which they were plunged, civilians had limited options. Self preservation and the defence of property were key concerns. Political and religious opinions existed, but caution and care were needed in the exercise of these. In this, both those loyal to George II and those of Jacobite sympathy were, in many ways, similar. However, the local status quo was stronger than the internal Jacobite threat; even in November 1745, the Ormskirk rising was crushed. It was only when the external force of the Jacobite army arrived that the civil forces were of limited use. Otherwise, loyalism could flourish unmolested. Loyalist demonstrations were mostly uninterrupted in 1745 or in 1746, which had not been the case between 1715 and 1716. Although Jacobitism of a kind was strong in the north west throughout much of the eighteenth century, in comparison, loyalism proved to be stronger and the former was both unwilling and incapable of effectively challenging it – even during times of extreme crisis, such as in 1745.

References

Introduction

1. R. Hopkinson, *Elections in Cumberland and Westmorland, 1695–1723* (Newcastle upon Tyne University PhD Thesis, 1973), 8.

2. P.G. Green, 'Samuel Peploe and the ideology of anti-Catholicism among the Anglican Clergy in early Hanoverian England,' *Lancashire and Cheshire Historical Society*, 145 (1996), 76–77.

3. G.H. Holmes and D. Szechi, *England in the Age of Oligarchy, 1722–1783* (London, 1993), 346–349.

4. Holmes and Szechi, *Oligarchy*, 381.

5. P. Rogers (ed.), *Daniel Defoe: A Tour through the Whole Island of Great Britain* (London, 1971), 540–541.

6. Ibid, 544–548.

7. Ibid, 548–549.

8. Ibid, 549; R. Patten, *History of the Late Rebellion* (London, 1717), 88.

9. Rogers, *Tour*, 550–551.

10. Szechi and Holmes, *Oligarchy*, 390.

11. Ibid, 381.

12. Rogers, *Tour*, 552, 557.

13. Ibid, 394–395.

14. R. Sedgwick, *The History of Parliament: The Commons, 1714–1754* (London, 1970).

15. Ibid, 221–223, 341–343, 268–274.

16. C.B. Phillips and J.H. Smith, *Lancashire and Cheshire from AD 1540* (London, 1994), 123.

17. N. McCord and R. Thompson, *The Northern Counties from AD 1000* (London, 1998), 164–165; Green, 'Peploe', 76–77.

18. E. Lord, *The Stuarts' Secret Army: English Jacobites, 1689–1752* (Harlow, 2004), 18–24.

19. Patten, *History*, 95.

20. TNA, KB8/66.

21. J.H. Hodson, *Cheshire, 1600–1780* (Chester, 1978) 22–24; P.K. Monod, *Jacobitism and the English people, 1689–1788* (Cambridge, 1989), 292–300; F P. Lole, 'A Digest of the Jacobite Clubs', *Royal Stuart Society Paper*, LV (1999).

22. Patten, *History*, 82–83.

23. Ibid, 86, 87.
24. P. Rae, *History of the Rebellion* (London, 1746), 317; W. Matthews (ed.), *The Diary of Dudley Ryder, 1715–1716* (London, 1939), 231, 234.
25. Patten, *History*, 89, 91.
26. C. Petrie, *The Jacobite Movement* (London, 1932), 195–206.
27. W.A. Speck, *The Butcher: The Duke of Cumberland and the Suppression of the Forty Five* (London, 1981); S. Reid, *1745: A Military History of the last Jacobite Rising* (Staplehurst, 1996); J. Black, *Culloden and the Forty Five* (Stroud, 1990); F. J. McLynn, *Bonnie Prince Charlie* (London, 1991); C. Duffy, *The '45* (London, 2003).
28. E. Cruickshanks, *Political Untouchables: The Tories and the '45* (London, 1978); Monod, *Jacobitism*; Lord, *Stuarts' Secret Army*.
29. F.J. McLynn, *The Final Campaign, 1745: The Jacobite Army in England* (Edinburgh, 1983.)
30. R.C. Jarvis, *Collected Papers on the Jacobite Risings* (Manchester University Press, 1971).
31. Ibid.
32. Ibid, *The Jacobite Risings of 1715 and 1745* (Carlisle, 1954).
33. G.C. Mounsey, *Carlisle in 1745* (Carlisle, 1846).
34. J.A. Wheatley, *Bonnie Prince Charlie in Cumberland* (Carlisle, 1903); J. Beattie, *Bonnie Prince Charlie in the Borderland* (1928).
35. J. Stirling, *The Jacobites in Lancashire* (Lancaster, 1971).
36. D. Higham, *Liverpool and the Forty Five* (Liverpool 1996).
37. R. Turner, 'Manchester in 1745', *Royal Stuart Society Paper*, XLIX (1997).
38. P.J.C. Smith, *The Invasion of 1745: The Drama in Lancashire and Cheshire* (Manchester, 1993).
39. Chancellor Ferguson, 'The Retreat through Westmorland in 1745', TCWAAS, Series One, X (1889), 186–228; D. Hepburn and C. Richardson, 'Documents relating to the transportation of cannon from Whitehaven to Carlisle during the Jacobite Rising of 1745', TCWAAS, Series Two, LXXXIV (1984), 141–166; J.D. Oates, 'The Last Siege on English Soil: Carlisle, 1745', TCWAAS, Series Three, III (2003), 169–184.
40. J.D. Oates, 'Sources for the Study of the Jacobite Rebellions of 1715 and 1745 in England', *The Local Historian*, 32, no. 3 (2002), 156–172.
41. J. Black (ed.), *British Politics and Society from Walpole to Pitt, 1742–1879* (London, 1994), 19.
42. McLynn, *Bonnie Prince Charlie*, 192.
43. Black, *Culloden and the Forty Five*, 132–133.
44. Speck, *The Butcher*, 195.
45. L. Colley, *Britons: Forging the Nation, 1707–1837* (Yale, 1992), 77.
46. Monod, *Jacobitism*, 6.
47. M.G.H. Pittock, *Jacobitism* (Aberdeen, 1998), 67–68.
48. D. Szechi, *The Jacobites, Britain and Europe, 1688–1788* (Manchester, 1994), 22.

Chapter One – Prelude to Invasion: September – October 1745

1.   TNA, SP36/69, f48r.
2.   TNA, SP36/69, f105r.
3.   TNA, SP36/70, f79v.
4.   Cruickshanks, *Political Untouchables*, 126–136.
5.   W.B. Blaikie (ed.), 'Origins of the Forty Five', *SHS*, series 2, no.2 (1916), 47.
6.   R.F. Bell (ed.), 'Memorials of John Murray of Broughton, 1740–*1747*', *SHS*, series 1, no.27 (1898), 103.
7.   Ibid, 451.
8.   TNA, SP36/69, f107r-109r.
9.   TNA, SP36/73, f33r.
10. TNA, SP36/67, f200v.
11. TNA, SP36/69, f22v.
12. TNA, SP36/71, f65r, 70, f207r, *MM*, 454, 1 October 1745.
13. British Library Additional Manuscripts, 32705, f.198r.
14. TNA, SP36/68, f243r.
15. Mounsey, *Carlisle*, 9.
16. G.C. Miller, *Hoghton Tower* (London, 1948), 116; J.H. Lumby (ed.), 'De Hoghton Deeds', *LCRS*, 88 (1936), 277.
17. P.C.Yorke (ed.), *The Life of Lord Chancellor Hardwicke*, I (Cambridge, 1913), 457.
18. TNA SP36/75, f89r-90v.
19. RA, CP 7/13.
20. Mounsey, *Carlisle*, 58.
21. TNA, SP36/67, f87r.
22. Miller, *Hoghton Tower*, 116.
23. BL. Add. Mss. 32705, f198r.
24. W. Brockbank and F. Kenworthy (eds.), 'The Diary of Richard Kay, 1716–1751', *CS*, (1968), 101.
25. *MM*, 447, 13 August 1745, 448, 20 August 1745, 449, 27 August 1745.
26. R.C. Jarvis, *The Jacobite Risings of 1715 and 1745* (Carlisle, 1954), 221–4.
27. Ibid, 230.
28. TNA, SP36/68, f243r.
29. Jarvis, *Collected Papers*, I, 116.
30. TNA, SP36/67, f.199r.
31. Jarvis, *Jacobite Risings*, 249–258.
32. TNA, SP36/68, f243r.
33. Lumby, 'De Hoghton Deeds', 280.
34. TNA, SP36/72, 156r, 73, 202v.
35. RA, CP 7/13.
36. TNA, SP36/73, f202v.
37. TNA, SP36/74, f187r.
38. TNA, SP36/69, f48r.
39. TNA, SP36/67, f199v-200v.
40. Miller, *Hoghton Tower*, 264.

41. LRO, DDHO/475/21.

42. Jarvis, *Jacobite Risings*, 230–1.

43. Ibid, 232–233.

44. TNA, SP36/68, f219r-220v.

45. TNA, SP36/69, f21v.

46. TNA, SP36/72, f94r.

47. CAS, Whitehaven, D/Pen. Acc.2689/14–15.

48. TNA, SP36/72, f234v; CAS, Whitehaven, D/Pen.Acc.2689/19; Jarvis, *Jacobite Risings*, 247n.

49. Jarvis, *Jacobite Risings*, 254.

50. TNA, SP36/68, f175r-177v.

51. TNA, SP36/68, f243r.

52. TNA, SP36/69, f126r.

53. *The Penny London Post*, 379, 30 September 1745 – 2 October 1745.

54. TNA, SP36/71, ff64v-64r.

55. TNA, SP36/71, ff64v-65r.

56. TNA, SP36/73, f202v.

57. TNA, SP36/69, f126r;Lumby, 'De Hoghton Deeds', 280.

58. R.J. Williamson, *Historical Records of the Regiment of Lancashire Militia* (London, 1876), 39.

59. *MM*, 454, 1 October 1745; LRO, DDK1741/7, Stanley to Derby 13 October 1745.

60. LRO, DDHO 389.

61. LRO, DDK/17141/7, Stanley to Derby, 13 October 1745.

62. TNA, SP36/68, f.206v-207v.

63. *GM*, 15 (1745), 554.

64. *The Westminster Journal*, 202, 12 October 1745.

65. RA, CP7/212.

66. *An Exact List of the Voluntary Subscribers* …(York, 1747), 26; *GM*, 15 (1745) 554; CA, DCH/X/9A/4.

67. LRO, PR2956/4/3; DDK1741/7.

68. Miller, *Hoghton Tower*, 117.

69. LRO, PR3168/7/9; PR2956/2/1; PR56.

70. CAS, Kendal, W/TE 3, 289.

71. CAS, Kendal, WPR32.

72. LRO, PR56.

73. Jarvis, *Jacobite Risings*, 249–270.

74. Ibid.

75. Lumby, 'De Hoghton Deeds', 281; Miller, *Hoghton Tower*, 117.

76. CA, DCH/X/9a/9; RA CP7/13.

77. TNA, SP36/73, f201v; Lumby, 'De Hoghton Deeds', 280, 282.

78. Miller, *Hoghton Tower*, 118.

79. Jarvis, *Jacobite Risings*, 245; TNA, SP36/73, f.241r.

80. CA, DCH/X/9a, Militia Order Book.

81. Mounsey, *Carlisle*, 4.

82. Ibid, *Carlisle*, 67; A.C. Ewald, *Life and times of Prince Charles Edward Stuart* (London, 1883), 152.
83. TNA, SP44/133, p.412.
84. TNA, SP36/68, f151r.
85. TNA, SP36/69, f105r
86. TNA, SP36/69, 270r.
87. TNA, SP36/70, f.49r.
88. TNA, SP36/69, f.105r.
89. TNA, SP36/70, f.78r-80v.
90. TNA, SP36/70, f.74r.
91. TNA, SP36/70, f49r.
92. CAS, Carlisle, Ca2/6, p.191.
93. Mounsey, *Carlisle*, 59.
94. Ibid; TNA, SP36/70, f.82r
95. TNA, SP36/70, f84r-86v.
96. CAS, Carlisle, Ca4/41.
97. Mounsey, *Carlisle*, 59, 72, 82.
98. CAS, Carlisle, Ca4/41.
99. Ibid.
100. Ibid.
101. Mounsey, *Carlisle*, 73.
102. TNA, SP36/70, f.244r
103. TNA, SP36/71, f270r; J.P. Dalton (ed.), 'Cumberland and the Forty Five, Some Letters', T*CWAAS*, Second Series, XLV (1946), 108.
104. TNA, SP36/68, f179r
105. TNA, SP36/68, f281r.
106. J. Ray, *Compleat History of the Rebellion* (London, 1754), 106.
107. MMM, DDX, 594, f1r-3r; TNA, SP44/132, 423.
108. *MM*, 455, 15 October 1745.
109. *London Evening Post*, 2793, 28 September – 1 October 1745.
110. TNA, SP36/69, f63r.
111. TNA, SP36/69, f84r.
112. TNA, SP36/70, f138r, 140r, 158r.
113. Jarvis, *Jacobite Risings*, 223.
114. Ibid, 224–225, 226–227.
115. Ibid, 224–7.
116. CAS, Kendal, WQ/o/6, WQ/1/6.
117. CAS, Whitehaven, D/Pen.Acc.2689/16–17.
118. CAS, Kendal, WD/TE Bound Vol.3, p.289; WPR32.
119. Miller, *Hoghton Tower*, 117.
120. Ibid, 120–121.
121. LRO, PR2956/2/1, PR56.
122. S. Peploe, *Popish Idolatory a Strong Reason why all Protestants should zealously oppose the present Rebellion…*(London, 1745) 3–16.
123. *GM*, 15 (1745), 554.

124. TNA, SP36/80, f475r.
125. Mounsey, *Carlisle*, 5–6.
126. BL, Additional Manuscripts, 32712, f29r.
127. Mounsey, *Carlisle*, 22.
128. Ibid, 72.
129. *The London Gazette*, 8478, 22–26 October 1745.
130. Mounsey, *Carlisle*, 30.
131. E. Hughes (ed.), *Fleming-Senhouse Papers* (Carlisle, 1961), 88.
132. Ibid, 89–90.
133. BL, ADD.MSS, 32712, f29r.
134. Mounsey, *Carlisle*, 58.
135. Ibid, 6, 8.
136. TNA, SP36/68, f47r, 255r; 69/108r, 272r; 70, 242r; 73, 150r.
137. TNA, SP36/73, f150r.
138. TNA, SP36/73, 208r.
139. Mounsey, *Carlisle*, 21.
140. TNA, SP36/71, f148r.
141. TNA, SP36/68, f153r.
142. *The General Evening Post*, 1874, 28 September – 1 October 1745; 1876, 3–5 October 1745; CA, DCH/X/9a/4.
143. H. Talon (ed.), *John Byrom: Selections form his Journal and Papers* (London, 1950), 225; *GM*, 15 (1745), 616; W.O. Roper, 'History of Lancashire', Part 1, *CS*, New Series, 61 (1907), p92.
144. TNA, SP36/68, f52r.
145. Mounsey, *Carlisle*, 62.
146. T. Maddox, *A Sermon preach'd at St. George's Church in Liverpool* (Liverpool, 1745), 3.
147. Ibid, 5–6, 11, 26–27, 30.
148. LRO, PR2905/2 /1; PR2956/2/1; PR2863/2/3; PR2067; PR2814/10.
149. CAS, Kendal, WPR/43/W1
150. CAS, Kendal, WPR8/W1.
151. T. Relph (ed.), *Arthuret and Longtown* (Published privately, 1997), 56–58.
152. *The Penny London Post*, 381, 7–9 October 1745.
153. Talon, *Byrom*, 225.
154. Miller, *Hoghton Tower*, 266.
155. CAS, Whitehaven, D/Pen. Acc.2689/10.
156. Bell, 'Murray' 239n.
157. *MM*, 453, 24 September 1745; 455, 15 October; 456, 22 October; 459, 12 November 1745
158. J.P. Earwaker (ed.), *The Constables' Accounts, III* (Manchester, 1892), 19.
159. *The Penny London Post*, 396, 8–11 November 1745.
160. Ibid, 397, 10–13 November 1745.
161. CAS, Carlisle, Ca4/41.
162. CAS, Carlisle, Ca4/42.
163. W.S. Lewis (ed.), *Horace Walpole's Correspondence: Walpole to Mann, 1742–1745*, vol. 18 (Yale, 1955), 408.

164. *The London Gazette*, 8470, 24–28 September 1745.

165. Ibid, 1–5 October 1745, 8472.

166. Ibid, 8478, 22–26 October 1745.

167. Ibid, 8478, 22–26 October 1745.

168. Brocksbank and Kenworthy, 'Richard Kay', 102.

169. TNA, SP36/72, f156r.

170. TNA, SP36/70, f140r.

171. *The Daily Post*, 8147, 6 October 1745.

Chapter Two – The Jacobite Invasion of England: November 1745

1. Bell, 'Memorials', 231–234.

2. TNA, SP36/69, f281r.

3. Elcho, Lord, *Short Account of the affairs of Scotland, 1744–1746* (Edinburgh. 1907), 301.

4. B. Rawson (ed.), The Chevalier de Johnstone: A *Memoir of the Forty Five* (London, 1972), 47.

5. Elcho, *Short Account*, 337.

6. Rawson, *Memoir*, 47; Elcho, *Short Account*, 310.

7. A. and H. Tayler (eds.), *1745 and After* (Edinburgh, 1938), 96n.

8. TNA, SP36/78, f92r-94r; Ewald, *Prince Charles Stuart*, 155–156.

9. TNA, SP36/78, f95r-97v.

10. Bell, *Memorials*, 451.

11. Wheatley, *Bonnie Prince Charlie*, 23–24.

12. Elcho, *Short Account*, 310.

13. Bell, 'Memorials', 239n.

14. Tayler, *1745 and after*, 95–96.

15. A. Henderson, *The History of the Rebellion* (Edinburgh, 1748), 55.

16. Lewis, *Correspondence, 19, Walpole to Mann*, III, 165–166.

17. Mounsey, *Carlisle*, 113.

18. Elcho, *Short Account*, 312–313; Henderson, *History*, 56.

19. Henderson, *History*, 55–56.

20. Mounsey, *Carlisle*, 74, 78, 53.

21. CAS, Whitehaven, Y/Pen.Acc. 2689/27.

22. CAS, Whitehaven, YD/Da.8.

23. TNA, SP36/74, f106r; CAS, Whitehaven, Y/Pen.Acc. 2689/27.

24. CAS, Whitehaven, Y/Pen.Acc. 2689/23.

25. TNA, SP36/76, f.16v.

26. Bell, *Memorials*, 241; CAS, Whitehaven, Y/Pen. Acc.2689/35.

27. CAS, Whitehaven, D/Pen/Acc.2689/35.

28. Mounsey, *Carlisle*, 114.

29. Lewis, *Walpole*, 165–6.

30. TNA, SP36/73, f360r.

31. Elcho, *Short Account*, 314; Taylers, *1745 and After*, 94.

32. CAS, Carlisle, Ca4/42.

33. TNA, SP36/81,f213r-218v.

34. Mounsey, *Carlisle*, 107–108, 110, 123.

35. RA, CP 7/62.

36. Mounsey, *Carlisle*, 56, 120.

37. Elcho, *Short Account*, 324.

38. J. Maxwell, *Narrative of the Expedition of Prince Charles Stuart* (London, 1841), 64–65.

39. TNA, SP36/76, f177r.

40. CAS, Whitehaven, DF/4/12.

41. Ray, *History*, 98

42. CAS, Kendal, WPR/8/W1.

43. CAS, Carlisle, PR5/31.

44. J. Hodgkinson, *The Greater Parish of Kendal, 1553–2002* (Kendal, 2002), 20.

45. Bell, 'Memorials', 243–244; Elcho, *Short Account*, 323.

46. Elcho, *Short Account*, 323.

47. Rawson, *Memoir*, 52.

48. Elcho, *Short Account*, 325.

49. *St. James' Evening Post*, 5598, 3–5 December 1745.

50. A. Livingstone, C.W.H. Aikman, B.S. Hart (eds.), *A Muster Roll of Prince Charles' Stuart's Army, 1745–1746* (Aberdeen, 1984), 194–199; J.G. Arnot and B.S. Seton, 'Prisoners of the Forty Five', *SHS*, 3rd series (1928–1929), 13–15; TNA, KB33/4/1.

51. CAS, Carlisle, D.Hud18/49/5.

52. TNA, TS20/112.1, 6.

53. CAS, Whitehaven, D/Pen.Acc.2689/18.

54. TNA, SP36/74, f161r-162v, 75, f36r.

55. TNA, SP36/74, f226r.

56. *The London Evening Post*, 2823, 7–9 December 1745; *General Evening Post*, 1902, 3–5 Dec. 1745; Dalton, *Cumberland and the '45*, 111.

57. CAS, Whitehaven, D/Pen.Acc.2689/34.

58. Ray, *History*, 119.

59. *GM*, 16 (1746), 235.

60. MMM, DX 594, f.2r.

61. MMM, DX 594, ff.3v-r.

62. TNA, SP36/69, f234v; MMM, DX 594, ff.3r-4r.

63. MMM, DX 594, ff.4r-5v.

64. BL, ADD.MSS 32705, f375r.

65. MMM, DX 594, ff.7v-r.

66. BL, ADD.MSS. 32705, f367r.

67. MMM, DX 594, ff.9v-10r.

68. MMM, DX 594, f.18v.

69. RA, CP7/142.

70. MMM, DX 594, f.13r.

71. MMM, DX 594, ff.14r-15v.

72. Ray, *History*, 109.

73. RA, CP7/112.
74. LRO, DDHO/475/56, 58, 63, 69, 74, 75, 80.
75. TNA, SP36/73, f186r-7v.
76. RA, CP 7/112.
77. RA, CP 7/112.
78. Miller, *Hoghton Tower*, 118–9; LRO, DDHO/1475/86.
79. CAS, Whitehaven, D/Pen.Acc.2689/32.
80. LRO, DDSC 44/15.
81. RA, CP7/113.
82. TNA, SP36/76, f157r-158v; Roper, 'Lancaster'. 88.
83. TNA, SP36/72, f.102r, 327r.
84. *HMC 35, Kenyon*, 482.
85. Ray, *History*, 125–6.
86. J.P. Earwaker (ed.), 'Manchester and the Rebellion of 1745', *LCAS*, 7 (1889), 147–8.
87. Jarvis, *Collected Papers*, I, 176–179.
88. *St. James' Evening Post*, 5597, 30 November – 3 December 1745; *The London Evening Post*, 2818, 26–28 November 1745.
89. Elcho, *Short Account*, 325–326.
90. H. Broxap, *A Biography of Thomas Deacon* (Manchester, 1911), 106.
91. J.P. Earwaker, *Constables' accounts*, 21–3; *HMC Kenyon*, 479–85.
92. *HMC Kenyon*, 480.
93. Ibid, 481.
94. Ibid, 480.
95. *The General Evening Post*, 1901, 30 November-3 December 1745.
96. Bell, 'Murray of Broughton', 245.
97. *The Penny London Post*, 404, 27–29 November 1745.
98. LRO, DDSc44/15; Talon, *John Byrom*, 226.
99. *The General Advertiser*, 3456, 26 November 1745.
100. Talon, *John Byrom*, 226.
101. *The Manchester Magazine*, 462, 24 December, 1745.
102. Brocksbank and Kenworthy, 'Richard Kay', 102.
103. Ibid.
104. *The True Patriot*, 4, 26 November 1745.
105. V.S. Doe (ed.), 'The Diary of James Clegg of Chapel en le Firth', II *Derbyshire Record Society*, (1979), 558.
106. Rawson, *Memoir*, 55.
107. Ibid, 55–56.
108. S. Markham (ed.), *John Loveday of Caversham* (London, 1984), 361.
109. Elcho, *Short Account*, 326.
110 I.G. Brown and H. Cheape (eds.), *Witness to Rebellion* (Edinburgh, 1996), 26.
111. Elcho, *Short Account*, 327.
112. A. and H. Tayler, *1745*, 98.
113. Bell, 'Memorials', 246.
114. Elcho, *Short Account*, 331n; *VCH Lancashire*, VIII, 78.

115. Anon, *A Genuine Account of the Behaviour, Confessions and dying words of Francis Townley* (London, 1746) 15–16.
116. Blaike, 'Origins', 167–8.
117. TNA, SP36.81, f208r.
118. H.W. Clemsha, *A History of Preston in Amounderness* (Manchester, 1912), 201.
119. Blaike, 'Origins', 168.
120. Talon, *John Byrom*, 230–231.
121. Markham, *John Loveday*, 361.
122. TNA, SP36/76, f157r.
123. *Elcho, Short Account*, p.327.
124. Ibid, 330.
125. Bell, 'Memorials', 246.
126. Blaikie, 'Origins', 169–170.
127. TNA, SP36/75, f87r.
128. RA, CP7/163.
129. *The Penny London Post*, 405, 29 November – 2 December; *The General Evening Post*, 1901, 30 November – 3 December 1745; TNA, SP36/75, f115r
130. *The Penny London Post*, 405, 29 November – 2 December 1745.
131. RA, CP7/212.
132. H. Tayler (ed.), *Jacobite Epilogue* (London, 1941), 149.
133. Tayler, 1745, 99n.
134. *GM*, 16 (1746), 324.
135. Blaikie, 'Origins', 169–170.
136. Brocksbank and Kenworthy, 'Richard Kay', 102.
137. Ibid.
138. Talon, *John Byrom*, 19.
139. Elcho, *Short Account*, 328.
140. Tayler, *1745*, 99.
141. Elcho, *Short Account*, 330.
142. Ibid, 331.
143. Lewis, *Walpole*, III, 179; J. Home, *History of the Rebellion* (Edinburgh, 1822), 105.
144. Livingstone, Aikman and Hart, *Muster Roll*, 194–199
145. Ibid.
146. *HMC Kenyon*, 476; ODNB 7, 236, 15, 614–616, 55, 113; TNA, KB33/4/1.
147. Arnot and Seton, 'Prisoners'.
148. ODNB 15, 614–616, 55, 113; Blaikie, 'Origins', 171.
149. *True Copies of the Papers wrote by Arthur Lord Balmerino…*, (Edinburgh, 1750), 32.
150. Elcho, *Short Account*, 331.
151. *The Penny London Post*, 422, 8–10 January 1746.
152. TNA, KB33/4/1.
153. TNA, TS20/89/2.
154. LRO, RCLN/9/1.

155. *GM*, 16 (1746),494–495.

156. Elcho, *Short Account*, 332–333.

157. Maxwell, *Narrative*, 22.

158. TNA, PL26/35/4; 36/1.

159. LRO, QSO2/115.

160. TNA, SP36/82, f54r.

161. W. Beaumont, 'Some Occurrences during the Rebellion of 1745 principally in Warrington and the Neighbourhood', LCAS, 2 (1849), 185.

162. TNA, SP36/81, f183r-184r.

163. W.H. Challoner (ed.), *The Autobiography of Samuel Bamford*, I (Cass, 1967), 18–19.

164. Ibid, 15–17.

165. TNA, SP36/81, f184r.

166. *GM* 16 (1746), 495.

167. Anon, *The Genuine Dying Speech of the Revd. Parson Coppock* (Carlisle, 1745), 22, 24–25; Anon, *The Authentic History of the Life and Character of Thomas Cappock* (London, 1750), 4, 10.

168. Anon, *True Copies of the Dying Declarations of Arthur, Lord Balmerino…*(Edinburgh, 1750) 44–48; *GM*, 16 (1746), 495.

169. Elcho, *Short Account*, 330–331.

170. A.A. Mumford, *Manchester Grammar School, 1515–1915* (London, 1919) 161–2; LRO, DDHO/1475/117.

171. *The Penny London Post*, 513, 8–11 August 1746.

172. Talon, *John Byrom*, n.61, 230–231.

173. Talon, *John Byrom*, 229, 231; TNA, SP36/81, f153v, 155r

174. Talon, *John Byrom*, 244.

175. ODNB, 15, 615; *GM* 16 (1746), 579–580.

176. Talon, *John Byrom*, 224.

177. Ibid, 232.

178. Elcho, *Short Account*, 333–334; CA, DCH/X/9a/13.

179. CA, ZAB4, f115v.

180. CA, Cowper MSS 1, 278.

181. CA, Cowper MSS, 1. 278.

182. CA, DCH/X/9A/9.

183. CA, DCH/X/9/A/9, 10.

184. TNA, SP36/73, f.255r.

185. RA, CP7/38.

186. RA, CP 7/100.

187. TNA, SP36/74, f.46r.

188. RA, CP7/21.

189. CA, Cowper MSS, 1, 279.

190. CA, DCH/X/9a/28.

191. TNA, SP 36/73, f.227r.

192. BL,ADD.MSS.32707, f411r.

193. TNA, SP36/80, f477r.

194. G.B. Crawford (ed.) 'The Diary of George Booth of Chester', *Chester and North Wales Archaeological Society*, 28 (1928), 71.
195. CA, P20/13/2.
196. TNA, SP36/75, f115v.
197. TNA, SP36/75, f37r.
198. CA, DCH/X/9a/13.
199. CA, Cowper, MSS, I, 279.
200. CA, P241/7/1.
201. CA, P77/8/1.
202. CA, P284/5063/18.
203. TNA, SP36/75, f37r.
204. TNA, SP36/75, f114r.
205. TNA, TS20/93/1, 3.
206. TNA, TS20/93/3.
207. F. Renaud, *History of Prestbury* (Manchester, 1876), 181; C.S. Davies, (ed.), *A History of Macclesfield* (Manchester, 1961), 111.
208. Elcho, *Short Account*, 334.
209. TNA, TS20/93/3.
210. Ray, *History*, 144.
211. Renaud, *Prestbury*, 178–179.
212. R. Chambers, *History of the Rebellion of 1745–6* (London, 1869), 188.
213. CA, QJB3/10 January 1746.
214. Arnot and Seton, 'Prisoners'.

Chapter Three – December 1745

1.   Ray, *History*, 152–153.
2.   Markham, *Loveday*, 362.
3.   Elcho, *Short Account*, 337.
4.   C. Duffy, *The '45* (London, 2003), 300–313.
5.   Blaikie, 'Origins', 177.
6.   Ray, *History*, 177.
7.   TNA, SP36/81, f298v.
8.   RA, CP8/17.
9.   CAS, Whitehaven, D/Pen.Acc.2689/41.
10. Roper, 'History of Lancashire', Part 1, 92.
11. TNA, TS 20/93/8; G. S. Taylor, ed., *The Life and Uncommon Adventures of Captain Dudley Bradstreet* (New York, 1954), 134.
12. Yorke, *Hardwicke*, I, 480.
13. Brocksbank and Kenworthy, 'Richard Kay' 103; Talon, *Byrom*, p.233.
14. Henderson, *History*, 63.
15. Maxwell, *Narrative*, 80
16. Ray, *History*, 179–182.
17. Maxwell, *Narrative*, 79–80.
18. Ray, *History*, 182; Elcho, *Short Account*, 345.

19.   Henderson, *History*, 63.
20.   Elcho, *Short Account*, 344; Talon, *Byrom*, 245.
21.   Talon, *Byrom*, 238–245.
22.   Earwaker, *Accounts*, 24.
23.   Talon, *John Byrom*, 235.
24.   Ibid.
25.   Parkinson, 'Remains', 401, 405, 417.
26.   Elcho, *Short Account*, 343.
27.   Blaikie, 'Origins', 180.
28.   Tayler, *1745*, 104.
29.   *HMC Var. Coll.*, VIII, 141.
30.   T.A. Coward, *Picturesque Cheshire* (London, 1903), 366.
31.   RA, CP8/6.
32.   Beaumont, 'Some Occurrences,' 191.
33.   CA, P85/10/1.
34.   CA, P14/3435/8/2.
35.   LRO, PR183.
36.   Taylor, *Dudley Bradstreet*, 134.
37.   Ibid, 134–135.
38.   Ibid, 136.
39.   RA, CP8/4.
40.   RA, CP8/22.
41.   RA, CP8/37a.
42.   RA, CP8/63.
43.   *MM*, 462, 24 December 1745.
44.   TNA, TS20/7/2.
45.   TNA, SP36/77, f52r.
46.   A. Saville ed., 'Secret Comment: The Diaries of Gertrude Saville, 1721–1757' *Thoroton Society*, Vol. 41 (1997), 263.
47.   Brocksbank and Kenworthy, 'Richard Kay' 103–4.
48.   TNA, SP36/79, f.290r; 80, 84v
49.   *The Penny London Post*, 414, 20–23 December 1745.
50.   Brocksbank and Kenworthy, 'Richard Kay', 105.
51.   Tayler, *Bradstreet,* 135.
52.   TNA, KB33/4/1.
53.   C.E. Whiting (ed.), 'Two Yorkshire Diaries', *YASRS*, 107 (1952), 117.
54.   Elcho, *Short Account*, 345.
55.   Blaikie, 'Origins', 181.
56.   Whiting, 'Two Yorkshire Diaries', 113.
57.   Ibid, 114.
58.   Talon, *John Byrom*, 236.
59.   Yorke, *Hardwicke*, I, 483.
60.   RA, CP8/57.
61.   RA, CP8/6.
62.   Blaikie, 'Origins', 179.

63. Rawson, *Memoir*, 75.
64. *HMC Var. Coll. VIII*, 147.
65. Elcho, *Short Account*, 347; Henderson, *History*, 64; Blaikie, 'Origins', 184.
66. CAS: Kendal, WPR38/6.
67. Blaikie, 'Origins', 184.
68. Ray, *History*, 186; Blaikie, 'Origins', 184–185; *GM*, 16 (1746), 301.
69. Elcho, *Short Account*, 347.
70. Henderson, *History*, 64.
71. Rawson, *Memoir*, 66; Home, *History*, 107; Elcho, *Short Account*, 347–348.
72. *GM*, 16 (1746), 301.
73. Ibid.
74. Dalton, 'Some Letters',112.
75. RA, CP8/17, 25.
76. *The Penny London Post*, 416, 25–27 December 1745.
77. RA, CP8/25.
78. Henderson, *History*, 64–65; *MM*, 463, 31 December 1746.
79. *Penny London Post*, 416, 25–27 December 1745.
80. RA, CP8/41.
81. *MM*, 467, 21 January, 1746.
82. Home, *History*, 107–108.
83. Ibid, 108–109.
84. C. Fergusson, 'The Retreat of the Highlanders through Westmorland in 1745' *TCWAAS*, Series One, X (1889), 210.
85. RA, CP8/102.
86. Ray, *History*, 185.
87. Ibid, 196.
88. Blaikie, 'Origins', 186–187.
89. Elcho, *Short Account*, 343.
90. Blaikie, 'Origins', 181; Jarvis, *Jacobite Risings*, 376–378.
91. Blaikie, 'Origins', 187.
92. Jarvis, *Jacobite Risings*, 319–325; *GM*, 16 (1746), 301.
93. Ray, *History*, 202.
94. MMM, DX 594, ff19r-31v.
95. Henderson, *History*, 68–69; RA, CP8/209.
96. Relph, *Diaries*, 60.
97. Ibid.
98. Doe, 'Clegg', II, 559.
99. Crawford, 'Diary of George Booth', 71.

Chapter Four – 1746 and After

1. Talon, *John Byrom*, 240–242.
2. Relph, *Diaries*, 61–62.
3. Brockbank and Kenworthy, 'Richard Kay', 105.
4. CAS, Carlisle, D/Sen/Fleming/15, Lonsdale – Lewis, 30 January 1746.

5.   LRO, DDHO475/99.
6.   Brockbank and Kenworthy, 'Richard Kay', 105.
7.   Ibid, 106.
8.   MMM, DX, f34v-40r.
9.   LRO, QSO2/115.
10. LRO, QSO2/115.
11. *GM*, 16 (1746), 105.
12. *The General Advertiser*, 3638, 24 June 1746.
13. CA, QJB3/10.
14. TNA, SP36/81, f152r-155r, 183r-184r, 213r-218v, TS20/93/1–5.
15. Lumby, 'De Hoghton Papers', 284–286.
16. *MM*, 479, 29 April 1746.
17. *GM*, 16 (1746), 325.
18. *The Penny London Post*, 422, 8–10 Jan. 1746; Wheatley, *Bonnie Prince Charlie*, 41.
19. CAS, D/Sen.14/3/16, Lowther – Fleming, 11 February 1746.
20. TNA, SP36/81, ff47r, 49r.
21. TNA, SP36/82, f245v.
22. *The Penny London Post*, 513, 8–11 August 1746; Jarvis, *Collected Papers*, II, 252; S. Hibbert-Ware, *History of the Foundations in Manchester*, II (London, 1834), 125.
23. *The Penny London Post*, 422, 8–10 Jan, 1746; Wheatley, *Bonnie Prince Charlie*, 41.
24. LRO, QSO2/115.
25. LRO, QSF 1565/2.
26. CA, QJB3/10.
27. CA, ZAB4, f119.
28. CA, ZAB4, f125.
29. Jarvis, *Jacobite Risings*, 275–289.
30. Seton and Arnot, 'Prisoners' I, 86.
31. *GM*, 16 (1746), 494–495, 554–555.
32. Ibid.
33. Ibid, 557, 610.
34. Ray, *History*, 427–428.
35. Arnot and Seton, 'Prisoners' I, 104, 108.
36. BL, ADD.MSS. 32707, f412r.
37. Relph, *Diaries*, 69–70.
38. Jarvis, *Collected Papers*, II, 263; Talon, *John Byrom*, 241–242.
39. TNA, SP36/85, f103v.
40. Seton and Arnot, eds., 'Prisoners of the Forty Five', I, 42, 46.
41. Roper, 'Lancaster', 99.
42. Talon, *Byrom*, 239.
43. *The Daily Post*, 8222, 1 January 1746.
44. Doe, 'Diary of James Clegg', Part 2, 562.
45. LRO, PR2905/2/1; PR2814/27.

46. Talon, Byrom, 242.
47. *The Westminster Journal*, 230, 26 April 1746.
48. *The General Advertiser*, 3586, 24 April 1746.
49. CA, P14/3435/8/2; P51/12/2.
50. LRO, DDHO475/105.
51. Brockbank and Kenworthy, 'Richard Kay', 109.
52. CAS, Carlisle, Ca4/42.
53. CA, ZTAB 5, f102.
54. CAS, Carlisle, PR5/31; Kendal, WPR18/W1
55. CAS, Kendal, WPR43/W1.
56. CAS, Kendal, WPR76.
57. CAS, Carlisle, PR110/75.
58. LRO, PR2067; PR2814/10.
59. Brockbank and Kenworthy, 'Richard Kay', 109, 114–5.
60. *The London Evening Post*, 2885, 1–3 May 1746.
61. *MM*, 479, 29 April 1746.
62. *GM*, 16 (1746), 579.
63. TNA, SP36/83, f175v.
64. *The London Gazette*, 8537, 17–20 May 1746.
65. Ibid, 8538, 20–24 May; 8540, 27–30 May; 8543, 7–10 June; 8558, 29 July – 2 August 1746.
66. Green, 'Samuel Peploe', 93.
67. Brockbank and Kenworthy, 'Richard Kay', 114.
68. Maddox, *A Sermon preach'd at St. George's Church in Liverpool* (Liverpool, 1746); J. Owen, *A Sermon preach'd at Rochdale on October the 9th, 1746* (London, 1746).
69. Maddox, *Sermon*, 5–7; Owen, *Sermon*, 4–5, 12, 25–27.
70. Maddox, *Sermon*, 17, Owen, *Sermon*, 27.
71. Owen, *Sermon*, 8.
72. Maddox, *Sermon* 18–19.
73. CA, ZTAB 5, f103v.
74. Brockbank and Kenworthy, 'Richard Kay', 114–5.
75. *MM*, 467, 21 January 1746.
76. Ibid, 467, 21 January 1746; 468, 28 January 1746.
77. Ibid, 471, 18 February 1746.
78. Ibid, 477, 8 April 1746.
79. Ibid, 527, 31 March 1747.
80. Ibid, 5 May 1747.
81. Brockbank and Kenworthy, 'Richard Kay', 124.
82. Ibid, 128.
83. Ibid, 114.
84. Broxap, *Thomas Deacon*, 188.
85. Information from Don Higham, 31 May 2004.
86. TNA, SP36/83, f341r-342v, *GM*, 16 (1746), 324.
87. F.O. Blundell, *Old Catholic Lancashire*, III (London, 1941), p.99.

88. CAS, Carlisle, D/Hud/18/9/1; Tayler, *Jacobite epilogue*, 149.

89. *The Penny London Post*, 426, 17–20 Jan. 1746.

90. Ibid, 420, 3–6 Jan. 1746.

91. *HMC Kenyon*, 487–490.

92. Brockbank and Kenworthy, 'Richard Kay', 115–6.

93. Broxap, *Thomas Deacon*, 124, 187.

94. *GM*, 16 (1746), 579.

95. TNA, PL, 26/35/4

96. TNA, PL, 26/35/5.

97. TNA, PL, 26/36/1.

98. Monod, *Jacobitism*, 202–203.

99. *GM*, 16 (1746), 579.

100. Ibid.

101. *MM*, 506, 4 November 1746.

102. TNA, PL26/36/1.

103. R.V.H. Burne, *Chester Cathedral* (London, 1958), 199–200.

104. A. Barton, *Rushbearing* (Manchester, 1891), 66–67.

105. *GM*, 16 (1746), 579–580.

106. Ibid, 689–691.

107. Ibid, 638.

108. Ibid, 17, 1747, 76.

109. TNA. TS20/37/8.

110. Hibbert-Ware, *Foundations*, 126, 129, 133.

111. Parkinson (ed.), 'Remains of Byrom', *Chetham Society*, 44 (1858), 2/2, 446, 509–510.

112. LRO, DDB74/13.

113. *The London Evening Post*, 3315, 28–31 January 1749.

114. Monod, *Jacobitism*, 200.

115. *Palatine Note Book*, III (1883), 277.

116. O. Mosley, *My Life* (London, 1968), 2; W.H. Thomson, *Beppy Byrom's Diary* (London, 1955), 8–12; Mumford, *Manchester Grammar School*, 233.

117. Parkinson, 'Remains', 469, 448.

118. Monod, *Jacobitism*, 298–300; Lole, 'Jacobite Clubs'.

119. Parkinson, 'Remains of Byrom', 628.

120. A. Oliver (ed.), *The Journal of Samuel Curwen, Loyalist*, I (Harvard, 1972), 366–367.

121. H.Walpole, *Memoirs of the reign of George II*, I, (London, 1847), p.17.

Conclusion

1. Ray, *Rebellion*, 155.

List of Abbreviations

BL British Library
CA Cheshire Archives
CAS Cumbria Archive Service
CP Cumberland Papers
CS Chetham Society
GM The Gentleman's Magazine
HMC Historic Manuscript Commission
KB King's Bench
LCHS Lancashire and Cheshire Historical Society
LCRS Lancashire and Cheshire Record Series
LRO Lancashire Record Office
MM The Manchester Magazine
MMM Merseyside Maritime Museum
ODNB Oxford Dictionary of National Biography
PL Palatinate of Lancashire
RA The Royal Archives
SHS Scottish Historical Society
SP State Papers
TCWAAS Transactions of the Cumberland and Westmorland
    Archaeological and Antiquarian Society.
TNA The National Archives
TS Treasury Solicitors
YASRS Yorkshire Archaeological Society Record Series

Bibliography

Published Primary Sources

Anon, *A Genuine Account of the Behaviour, Confessions and dying words of Francis Townley* (London, 1746).

Anon, *The Genuine Dying Speech of the Revd. Parson Coppock* (Carlisle, 1745).

Anon, *The Authentic History of the Life and Character of Thomas Cappock* (London, 1750).

Anon, *True Copies of the Dying Declarations of Arthur, Lord Balmerino…*(Edinburgh, 1750).

R.F. Bell (ed.), 'Memorials of John Murray of Broughton, 1740–1747', SHS, 27 (1898).

W.B. Blaikie (ed.), 'A True Account of Mr John Daniels' Progress' in 'Origins of the Forty Five', SHS, series 2, no.2 (1916), 165–224.

W. Brockbank and F. Kenworthy (eds.), 'The Diary of Richard Kay, 1716–1751', *CS*, (1968).

I.G. Brown and H. Cheape (eds.), *Witness to Rebellion* (Edinburgh, 1996).

W.H. Challoner (ed.), *The Autobiography of Samuel Bamford*, I, (Cass, 1967).

R. Chambers, *History of the Rebellion of 1745–6* (London, 1869).

G.B. Crawford (ed.) 'The Diary of George Booth of Chester', *Chester and North Wales Archaeological Society,* 28 (1928), 5–96.

J.P. Dalton (ed.), 'Cumberland and the Forty Five, Some Letters', TCWAAS, Series Two, XLV (1946), 108–115.

V.S. Doe (ed.), 'The Diary of James Clegg of Chapel en le Firth', II *Derbyshire Record Society*, (1979).

J.P. Earwaker (ed.), 'Manchester and the Rebellion of 1745', *LCAS*, 7 (1889).

J.P. Earwaker (ed.), *The Constables' Accounts, III* (Manchester, 1892).

Elcho, Lord, *A Short Account of the Affairs of Scotland, 1744–1746* (Edinburgh, 1907).

A. Henderson, *The History of the Rebellion* (Edinburgh, 1748).

HMC 35: Kenyon.

J. Home, *History of the Rebellion* (Edinburgh, 1822).

E. Hughes (ed.), *Fleming-Senhouse Papers* (Carlisle, 1961).

R.C Jarvis (ed.), *The Jacobite Risings of 1715 and 1745* (Carlisle, 1954).

W.S. Lewis (ed.), *Correspondence of Horace Walpole, vols., 18 and 19, Walpole to Mann*, II and III (Yale, 1955).

J.H. Lumby (ed.), 'Appendix II The Jacobite Rebellions', in 'Houghton Deeds', LCRS, 88 (1936), 276–286.

T.Maddox, *A Sermon preach'd at St. George's Church in Liverpool* (Liverpool, 1746).

S. Markham (ed.), *John Loveday of Caversham* (London, 1984).

W. Matthews (ed.), *The Diary of Dudley Ryder, 1715–1716* (London, 1939).

J. Maxwell, *Narrative of the Expedition of Prince Charles* (London, 1841).

G.C. Miller, *Hoghton Tower* (London, 1948).

O. Mosley, *My Life* (London, 1968).

G.C. Mounsey, *Carlisle in 1745* (Carlisle, 1846).

J.D. Oates and K. Navickas (eds.) 'Jacobites and Jacobins', *Record Society of Lancashire and Cheshire*, forthcoming publication, (2006).

S. Oliver (ed.), *The Journal of Samuel Curwen, Loyalist*, I (Harvard, 1972).

J. Owen, *A Sermon preach'd at Rochdale on October the 9th, 1746* (London, 1746).

R. Parkinson (ed.), 'Remains of Byrom', CS, 44 (1858), 2/2.

R. Patten, *History of the Late Rebellion* (London, 1717).

S. Peploe, *Popish Idolatory a Strong Reason why all Protestants should zealously oppose the present Rebellion…*(London, 1745).

P. Rae, *History of the Rebellion* (London, 1746).

B. Rawson (ed.), *The Chevalier de Johnstone: A Memoir of the Forty Five* (London, 1972)

J. Ray, *Compleat History of the Rebellion* (London, 1754).

T. Relph (ed.), *Arthuret and Longtown* (Published privately, 1997).

P.Rogers (ed.), *Daniel Defoe: A Tour through the Whole Island of Great Britain* (London, 1971).

A. Saville (ed.), 'Secret Comment: The Diaries of Gertrude Saville, 1721–1757' *Thoroton Society*, Vol. 41 (1997).

H. Talon (ed.), *John Byrom: Selections form his Journal and Papers* (London, 1950).

A. and H. Tayler (eds.), *1745 and after* (Edinburgh, 1938).

H. Tayler (ed.), *Jacobite Epilogue* (London, 1941).

G. S. Taylor (ed.), *The Life and Uncommon Adventures of Captain Dudley Bradstreet* (New York, 1954).

W.H. Thomson (ed.), *Beppy Byrom's Diary* (London, 1955).

H.Walpole, *Memoirs of the reign of George II*, I (London, 1847).

C.E. Whiting (ed.), 'Two Yorkshire Diaries', YASRS, 107 (1952).

P.C.Yorke (ed.), *The Life of Lord Chancellor Hardwicke*, I (Cambridge, 1913).

Secondary Sources

J.G. Arnot and B.S. Seton, 'Prisoners of the Forty Five', SHS, 3rd series, 13–15, (1928–1929).

A. Barton, *Rushbearing* (Manchester, 1891).

J. Beattie, *Bonnie Prince Charlie in the Borderland* (1928).

W. Beaumont, 'Some Occurrences during the Rebellion of 1745 principally in Warrington and the Neighbourhood', LCAS, 2 (1849), 184–200.

J. Black, *Culloden and the Forty Five* (Stroud, 1990).

J. Black (ed.), *British Politics and Society from Walpole to Pitt, 1742–1789* (London, 1994).

H. Broxap, *A Biography of Thomas Deacon* (Manchester, 1911).

R.V.H. Burne, *Chester Cathedral* (London, 1958).

H.W. Clemsha, *A History of Preston in Amounderness* (Manchester, 1912).

L. Colley, *Britons: Forging the Nation, 1707–1837* (Yale, 1992).

T.A Coward, *Picturesque Cheshire* (London, 1903).

E. Cruickshanks, *Political Untouchables: The Tories and the '45* (London, 1978).

C.S. Davies (ed.), *A History of Macclesfield* (Manchester, 1961).

C. Duffy, *The '45* (London, 2003).

A.C. Ewald, *Life and times of Prince Charles Edward Stuart* (London, 1883)

Chancellor Ferguson, 'The Retreat through Westmorland in 1745', TCWAAS, Series One, X (1889), 186–228.

P.G. Green, 'Samuel Peploe and the ideology of anti-Catholicism among the Anglican Clergy in early Hanoverian England,' *LCHS*, 145 (1996), 75–94.

D. Hepburn and C. Richardson, 'Documents relating to the transportation of cannon from Whitehaven to Carlisle during the Jacobite Rising of 1745', TCWAAS, Series Two, LXXXIV (1984), 141–166.

S. Hibbert-Ware, *History of the Foundations in Manchester*, II (London, 1834).

D. Higham, *Liverpool and the Forty Five* (Liverpool 1995).

J.H. Hodson, *Cheshire, 1600–1780* (Chester, 1978).

J. Hodgkinson, *The Greater Parish of Kendal, 1553–2002* (Kendal, 2002).

G.H. Holmes and D. Szechi, *England in the Age of Oligarchy, 1722–1783* (London, 1993).

R. Hopkinson, *Elections in Cumberland and Westmorland, 1695–1723* Unpublished Newcastle upon Tyne University PhD Thesis (1973).

R.C. Jarvis, *Collected Papers on the Jacobite Risings* (Manchester University Press, 1971).

A. Livingstone, C.W.H. Aikman, B.S. Hart (eds.), A *Muster Roll of Prince Charles' Stuart's Army, 1745–1746* (Aberdeen, 1984).

P. Lole, 'A Digest of Jacobite Clubs', *Royal Stuart Society Papers*, XLV (1999).

E. Lord, *The Stuarts' Secret Army: English Jacobites, 1689–1752* (Harlow, 2004).

N. McCord and R. Thompson, *The Northern Counties from AD 1000* (London, 1998).

F. J. McLynn, *Bonnie Prince Charlie* (London, 1991).

F.J. McLynn, *The Final Campaign, 1745: The Jacobite Army in England* (Edinburgh, 1983.)

P. K. Monod, *Jacobitism and the English people, 1689–1788* (Cambridge, 1989).

A.A. Mumford, *Manchester Grammar School, 1515–1915* (London, 1919)

A.L. Murray, *The Royal Grammar School, Lancashire* (Cambridge nd.).

J. Oates, *Responses in the North east of England to the Jacobite Rebellions of 1715 and 1745*, unpublished University of Reading PhD thesis (2001).

J.D. Oates, 'The Last Siege on English Soil: Carlisle, 1745', TCWAAS, Series Three, III (2003), 169–185.

J.D. Oates, 'Sources for the Study of the Jacobite Rebellions of 1715 and 1745 in England', *The Local Historian*, 32, no. 3, (2002), 156–172.

J.D. Oates, 'Responses in the North of England to the Jacobite Rebellion of 1715', *Northern History*, XLIII:I (2006).

Palatine Note Book, III (1883).

C. Petrie, *The Jacobite Movement* (London, 1932).

C.B. Phillips and J.H. Smith, *Lancashire and Cheshire from AD 1540* (London, 1994).

M.G.H Pittock, *Jacobitism* (Aberdeen, 1998).

S. Reid, *1745: A Military History of the last Jacobite Rising* (Staplehurst, 1996).

F. Renaud, *History of Prestbury* (Manchester, 1876).

W.O. Roper, 'History of Lancashire', Part 1, CS, New Series, 61 (1907).

P. J.C. Smith, *The Invasion of 1745: The Drama in Lancashire and Cheshire* (1993)

R. Sedgwick, *The History of Parliament: The Commons, 1714–1754* (London, 1970).

W.A. Speck, *The Butcher: The Duke of Cumberland and the Suppression of the Forty Five* (London, 1981).

J. Stirling, *The Jacobites in Lancashire* (Lancaster, 1971).

D. Szechi, *The Jacobites, Britain and Europe, 1688–1788* (Manchester, 1994).

VCH Lancashire, VIII.

R. Turner, 'Manchester in 1745', *Royal Stuart Society*, XLIX (1997).

J.A. Wheatley, *Bonnie Prince Charlie in Cumberland* (Carlisle, 1903).

R.J. Williamson, *Historical Records of the Regiment of Lancashire Militia* (London, 1876).

Index

Occasional Papers from the Centre for North-West Regional Studies

The Centre for North-West Regional Studies, based at Lancaster University, brings together members of the University and the regional community. As well as its extensive publication programme of Occasional Papers and Resource Papers, the Centre organises conferences, study days and seminars covering a wide range of subjects. For a small annual subscription 'Friends of the Centre' receive regular mailings of events and discounts on books and other activities

For further details contact Centre for North-West Regional Studies, Fylde College, Lancaster University, Lancaster, LA1 4YF
Tel: 01524 593770; Fax: 01524 594725
Email: christine.wilkinson@lancaster.ac.uk   Website: www.lancs.ac.uk/users/cnwrs/

The Jacobite Invasion of 1745 in the North West (2006) Jonathan D. Oates, £12.95

Thomas Harrison, Georgian Architect of Chester and Lancaster, 1744–1829 (2005) John Champness, £12.50

Romans and Briton in North West England (third revised and extended edition) (2004) David Shotter, £13.50

Stained Glass from Shrigley and Hunt of Lancaster and London (2003) William Waters, £26.95

Transforming Fell and Valley (2003) Ian Whyte, £11.50

Walking Roman Roads in Lonsdale and the Eden Valley (2002) Philip Graystone, £10.95

The Wray Flood of 1967 (2002) Emmeline Garnett, £10.95

A Fylde Country Practice (2001) Steven King, £10.95

Irish Women in Lancashire (2001) Sharon Lambert, £9.95

Hadrian's Wall: A Social and Cultural History (2000) Alison Ewin, £8.50

Furness Abbey: Romance, Scholarship and Culture (2000) Christine Dade-Robertson, £11.50

Rural Industries of the Lune Valley (2000) ed. Michael Winstanley, £9.95

The Romans at Ribchester (2000) B. J. N. Edwards, £8.95

The Buildings of Georgian Lancaster (revised edition) (2000) Andrew White, £6.95

A History of Linen in the North West (1998) ed. Elizabeth Roberts, £6.95

History of Catholicism in the Furness Peninsula (1998) Anne C. Parkinson, £6.95

Vikings in the North West – The Artifacts (1998) B. J. N. Edwards, £6.95

Sharpe, Paley and Austin, A Lancaster Architectural Practice 1836–1952 (1998) James Price, £6.95

Victorian Terraced Housing in Lancaster (1996) Andrew White and Mike Winstanley, £6.95

Walking Roman Roads in the Fylde and the Ribble Valley (1996) Philip Graystone, £5.95

Romans in Lunesdale (1995) David Shotter and Andrew White, £6.50

Roman Route Across the Northern Lake District, Brougham to Moresby (1994) Martin Allan, £5.95

Walking Roman Roads in East Cumbria (1994) Philip Graystone, £5.95

St Martin's College, Lancaster, 1964–89 (1993) Peter S. Gedge and Lois M. R. Louden, £5.95

From Lancaster to the Lakes: the Region in Literature (1992) eds Keith Hanley and Alison Millbank, £5.95

Windermere in the Nineteenth Century (1991) ed. Oliver M. Westall, £4.95

Richard Marsden and the Preston Chartists (1981) J. E. King, £3.95

Each of these titles may be ordered by post from the above address. Postage and packing is £1.00 per order. Please makes cheques payable to 'The University of Lancaster'. Titles are also available from all good booksellers in the region.